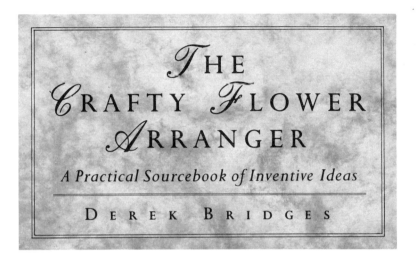

THE CRAFTY FLOWER ARRANGER

A Practical Sourcebook of Inventive Ideas

DEREK BRIDGES

Photography by Trevor Richards

CENTURY
London Sydney Auckland Johannesburg

Dedicated to the three I love best –
Pat, Sara and Paul

Text copyright © Derek Bridges 1989
Photographs copyright © Trevor Richards 1989
All rights reserved
First published in Great Britain in 1989
by Century Hutchinson Ltd, Brookmount House,
62-65 Chandos Place, Covent Garden, London WC2N 4NW

Century Hutchinson Australia Pty Ltd, 89-91 Albion Street,
Surry Hills, Sydney, New South Wales 2010, Australia

Century Hutchinson New Zealand Limited, PO Box 40-086,
Glenfield, Auckland 10, New Zealand

Century Hutchinson South Africa (Pty) Ltd, PO Box 337,
Bergvlei, 2012 South Africa

Book design by Bob Hook
Edited by Susan Fleming

Set in Perpetua by
SX Composing Ltd, Rayleigh, Essex
Printed and bound in Spain by Printer Industria Grafica SA, Barcelona

British Library Cataloguing in Publication Data

Bridges, Derek
The crafty flower arranger.
1. Flower arrangement
I. Title II. Richards, Trevor
745.92

ISBN 0 7126 2204 7

CONTENTS

INTRODUCTION

ou may well ask what on earth does he mean by the *crafty* flower arranger? Is it 'cunning', 'shrewd' or 'good with the hands'? Well, to be perfectly honest, it's all three. By the very nature of their calling, flower arrangers – whether professional like me, or enthusiastically amateur – are possessed of cunning, shrewdness and agile fingers. The first two qualities are particularly useful for those flower arrangers who enter competitions because, regardless of what many say, everyone enters to win, and only a crafty imagination can create something – colour combination, container, effect – that is a one-off, quite different from all the other offerings.

Flower arrangers are also good with their hands – they are, after all, continually handling delicate plant materials, whether fresh, dried or artificial, and creating wonderful shapes and effects within a limited area. I've been flower arranging for over twenty years, but I have also been practising – with enormous pleasure, I might say – many other crafty arts and skills. Following the success of *The Flower Arranger's Bible*, and the pleas of many listeners and readers for more intensive 'how-to' information, I thought I would like to share with you some of my 'craft' work, work that is related to, and will enhance, your flower arranging.

For *The Crafty Flower Arranger* takes the traditional skills of the flower arranger one step further. Using the same principles of colour, shape and design, I tell you how to create 'arrangements' of and in your garden, for instance, and how to create 'arrangements' on various surfaces using the principles of collage work. I tell you how to make that extra special container that might win you the best in show, and how to adapt and transform containers both for inside and outside. You'll be astonished at some of the concepts and amused by others, ranging as they do from perhaps the outrageously creative to what some people would simply term outrageous!

Some of these concepts might also seem to drift a little too far from flower arranging proper, but if you think about it, *anything* can be used as container, background or accessory for your art. Decorating a welcome ring for Christmas is as much a part of flower arranging as that magnificent grouping of fresh or dried materials in your hall, and it's only a small distance from decorating boxes, baskets, hats and heads. Finding – or adapting – just the right container for a group of foliage shrubs in your garden is as much flower arranging as a 'still-life' involving 'collected' or 'made' accessories in combination with flowers.

Crafty flower arrangers need to have an 'eye' for things that could be useful to them, and *my* 'eye' has led me in some quite unusual directions over the years. I must have been born with a peculiarly inventive mind, but I think that many of the ideas here will help you, too, to begin to see the present or future possibilities of even the most unlikely objects. Another quality of the crafty flower arranger is the magpie instinct, again related to the 'eye'; my own home – or rather my storage loft – is packed with items I have been collecting since I was old enough and bright enough to pick up a pretty shell. And the collecting involved need not be too taxing on your purse either: many items useful to us cost little or nothing.

I hope that this book will open your eyes to a multitude of ways in which you can expand your flower-arranging skills and your decorative instincts. I hope to inspire you, to get your mind working and your fingers busy, to make things of beauty as only you know how.

Derek Bridges, January 1989

Chapter One

THE CRAFTY GARDENER

*Y*ou may wonder why I have started this book with the garden, but, when you think about it, where would we flower arrangers be without our gardens? The two just go hand in hand. You can always tell flower arrangers' gardens by the things grown in them, for it's not usually flowers. These can always be bought from the florist, but it's the foliage, berries and seed heads that are less easy to come by, and these are the staples of a flower arranger's garden.

What is it, apart from the plants themselves though, that makes the 'different' garden different? I think it is the overall *look* of the garden, the different points of interest, and the groupings not only of plants, but of other objects. One of the most basic constituents of a massed flower arrangement, for instance, is the use of a variety of shapes and sizes of flowers and foliages to create interest – spikes, flats and rounds. This basic idea should also be applied to the flower arranger's garden, perhaps the largest massed arrangement you can ever attempt! My own garden is not what you would call big (the main comment from people who visit it), but it is full of points of interest, and again it's not always the plants that create them. These focal points can be many things, and I aim to introduce you to a few.

(Previous page) A selection of garden containers in my own collection: old bread pancheons to the left, various types of chimney pots to the right and back, a couple of wonderfully shaped ewers to the front and, overflowing with ivy, an 'antiqued' plastic garden-centre urn.

'Arranging' a Crafty Garden

First of all, it's a matter of that all-seeing eye which flower arrangers develop. Look closely at what you have to start with but, let's face it, we're not attempting to do a Capability Brown. Whether your garden is the size of two paving stones, or something that needs a sit-on mower, it doesn't matter, the principles are the same. Stand in various positions in the garden, and decide what you need

and what can be done: where does that corner catch the
sun, or what do you want to look at whilst doing the
washing up? Is there a bare wall that needs prettying up, or
something to be hidden from view? A group of mixed
conifers, for instance, is not only a wonderful foil for flower
arrangers' plants, but could serve as a wind-break, a
disguise for the dustbins or, better still, for that secret seat
where you flop when work is done. (I might tell you that I
have such a place in *my* garden, known as Gin and Tonic
Corner, which has become very famous.)

Creating Points of Interest

Once you have grasped the basic potential inherent in your
own garden, you can set about creating all those crafty
points of interest. I'm a great fan of container growing in
gardens, with which you can achieve groupings difficult to
effect in other ways – a multitude of sizes, shapes and
levels. Don't be too conventional in your choice of
containers either: there are a large number of less usual
items which can be used in the crafty garden (and you can
'fake up' some of them), as well as finds such as interesting
pieces of wood: large or small, these can be used either as a
visual effect on their own, or with a plant or two added to
make a 'garden arrangement'.

As I said, a planned garden is a massed arrangement in
itself, so it's perfectly feasible to create other 'arrangements'
within it – either against or on an interesting background,
or hanging on a wall. Any garden is ripe for the inclusion of
a number of crafty ideas, and I think you will see quite a
few in the following pages.

GARDEN CONTAINERS

When talking about containers for garden plants, the
problem is where to start. Containers abound in good
garden centres, but many I wouldn't give garden room to,
whereas on visits to Spain, I've seen so many containers
with garden potential that I'd need my own jumbo jet to
bring them back in! However, there are lots of alternatives
available here, some being other people's cast-offs, some
very crafty 'fakes'.

You may wonder why I so love growing in containers
when I have a garden, the ultimate 'container'. Growing in
containers can make for a garden which can be 'on the
move'; every year or season, you could swap suitable
containers or container groupings around from place to
place to have constant variety (not so easy with beds and
rockeries!). Most importantly, though, containers can
provide different surfaces, textures, shapes, lifts, levels and
interest, all of which I consider vital to the flower
arranger's crafty garden. Those containers displayed on
pages 8–9 are but a small selection from my own collection,
and from what is freely available to you all.

The first thing to do when looking for garden containers
is to 'match' them to your garden. If the layout is
geometrically modern, the gothic lines of an urn might not
suit; similarly, if the feel is cottagey, a modern container
would look out of place. However, many modern containers
can be made to *look* old (see page 18). Also consider the
type of plant you wish to put *in* the chosen containers: will
they suit the container's lines, and will the container be big
enough to actually *contain* the plant? Remember that plants
do grow: even if you keep sneaking off the odd branch or
leaf, the root action continues to get bigger.

Chimney Pots

Containers always look better when grouped together – that
focal point again – and I think you'll have to agree with me
if you look at the collection of chimney pots on page 15.
These are being taken down, mainly from Victorian houses,
now that central heating is being installed and open fires
banished. They can still be found fairly cheaply if you're
lucky, although the better looking and better preserved
ones have become the province of junk and antique shops.
And did you know that they're named after chess pieces?
There are kings and queens, etc., which is why there's such
an interesting variety of shapes and sizes.

Containers such as these are ideal, I think, for people
with limited ground space as they don't take up much
room, but I don't like to see a pair standing one either side
of the door, for instance, on sentry duty. Some are narrow-
mouthed, some wider, and this will dictate how you can fill
them and with what (see the *Tip* below). In the larger,
open-mouthed chimney pots, I would recommend that you
design the contents rather like a *pot de fleurs:* an ivy at the
front, a dwarf conifer or cypress at the back with space in
the middle for seasonal things; bulbs in the spring,
geraniums in the summer and a pot chrysanthemum in the
autumn. Thus you will have interest and variety going all
the time (see also page 143 for a list of suitable plants).

T I P

No, you don't need to fill the chimney pot with 3 cwt
of soil! You wedge an old plastic bucket with some holes
drilled in the bottom into the mouth of the pot. The
soil goes in this. When and if you want to move the
container, the bucket can be lifted out and both moved
separately. (Or use a wire hanging basket.)

(Far right) I have been using chimney pots as lifts and levels in my garden for some 17 years, and I think they're fantastic containers. Against the ivy-covered wall here, I think the three ivies in the three pots create a lovely little green oasis. Imagine this in the corner of a small back yard, hiding the dustbins for instance — much more interesting than a piece of lattice fencing!

(Right) I think there's nothing more attractive in a garden than the lovely little areas that can be created with these wonderful troughs (some genuine, some 'antiqued'). I love the idea of using a different texture — here the pebble backing — to show off a particular item. As you can see, the troughs are of different sizes and shapes, and some have been lifted on to boulders or bricks to add height. Fill them with spreading plants, or create a mini Alpine garden (see page 143).

Pancheons

These are those old bread mixing bowls which are dull yellow inside, dark brown outside (see the photograph on pages 8–9). I think they're fantastic containers – still available quite cheaply – as they're such a good shape for a plant group, with that wide open neck. You can drill a few holes in the bottom for drainage if you like (see the *Tip* opposite), but I don't do this, as I use them mainly as a container for my hostas (plantain lilies). These, as most of you will know, are bog plants basically, loving their feet in moisture while in leaf. So I simply put in broken crocks for basic drainage, à good potting compost, and then the plants, and I've had my two major hostas (the 'Albopicta' variety) in a pair of matching pancheons on the edge of a step for 16 years or so – *without* taking them out or dividing them. As you can imagine, there's not much soil left now – it's all root – so I make sure I give them a liquid feed once a week during the summer months when they're in all their glory, as well as a bucket of water a day. (You can't put a plant into one of these containers for all those years and not give them something to live on.)

From the Plumber's Yard

This is where you can find many a treasure for use as a garden container. Yes, I do mean the loo and cistern: I know of one loo group that looks fantastic during the summer months, overflowing with geraniums and ivies. They have very interesting shapes, and you can often find old ones which have decorative mouldings on them or patterns in a different colour. Even the chamber pot itself could be perched on a windowsill and filled with plants (use plenty of broken crocks or gravel for drainage). None of them needs be in perfect condition, as the plants will hide chips, and natural (or unnatural) garden ageing will diminish colour and hide cracks. None of them ought to be too expensive either; often the plumber will be glad to see the back of them.

Much more interesting, though, are the old white pot sinks which are carted off by the plumber when he installs your enamel or stainless steel alternative. These pot sinks make wonderful plant containers, mainly because they are deep, and have a ready-made drainage hole. You may demur at the idea of having a bright white sink in the middle of your garden – but you don't leave it white, you 'antique' it (see page 18). Thus you can create for yourself the equivalent of one of those lovely, virtually unobtainable, and extremely expensive York stone troughs. In the photograph on page 14, you will see that I have quite a collection, only a small selection of which I have grouped together against a pebble background. Some of these *are* genuine and old, but others are not, having been white pot sinks as recently as five years ago! If you look too at the picture on page 21, the stone urn has taken on a wonderful age: it was done only 12 years ago, but looks wonderfully ancient, and I defy anybody to differentiate the real from the fake.

T I P

If you're worried that broken crocks won't supply enough drainage in a container like a pancheon, simply drill a couple of drainage holes in the sides about 5 cm (2 inches) up from the base. Make the holes large enough to take an old wine cork. Let water seep through the soil, and, if you feel there's some waterlogging, take out the wine cork bungs until the surplus has run away, then replace.

'ANTIQUING' GARDEN
CONTAINERS

Not everyone has the time or money to seek out genuinely old and antique-looking containers for the garden – they do take some finding – but there are modern cement-type versions available at garden centres – tubs, boxes, pots, urns, etc. These, if left outside to weather naturally for several months, can begin to look quite good, but if you want to create a virtually instant 'aged' look, you will have to resort to craftiness. You can use a variety of substances, some of which are comparatively pleasant, some which are positively unpleasant (see the *Tip* below)!

T I P

To create antiquity naturally and swiftly on concrete-style containers, you can paint on a mixture of plain yoghurt and water: this attracts the atmosphere, algae and mosses very quickly, and can look good within weeks. Another idea is perhaps less pleasant. If you have the stamina, collect from the fields what the cows have left behind, mix again with water, and paint over the new-looking container. Your friends won't be around for a while perhaps, but your containers will start to look better! (Both these ideas are effective, too, on a new bit of brickwork that does not match the old.)

But for most modern containers – cement-style or plastic – or the white pot sinks I mentioned above, you need a more thorough antiquing treatment. It's not difficult, although it may sound complicated, and all the materials can be obtained fairly easily. You will need a tin of Polybond – a lovely, tacky glue-like substance – from your DIY shop; sand, cement and peat; water, a 'stirrer' (I use a stick), an old bucket, paintbrush and scrubbing or shoe brush. If you're working on a pot sink, set it up where you want it to stay (they're not quite so easy to lift), and cover the ground with a groundsheet or layers of newspaper – it's a very clarty job you're embarking on. If working on an urn, you could contain the mess as I have done in the illustrations below, by placing the urn inside a cardboard box.

You can then proceed as I've described in the drawings and captions below. When you've finished, let it stand for at least a couple of days before you do any planting. In fact, I think it's best to do this antiquing on a container early on

---

1. With your paintbush, apply the Polybond on to the urn in sections – I'm probably working on an area here of about 30 x 23 cm (12 x 9 inches). (If the section is too big, the Polybond will be dry before you can affix all the mixture.) While this small section becomes tacky, make up your 'antique' mix.

2. Mix together equal parts of sand, cement and peat in an old bucket. It will look like a good Christmas pudding mix. Add enough water to make it hold together when you pick up a tennis ball-sized handful. It should not be too wet or sloppy. Pick up handfuls and press them on to the Polybonded area of the urn.

3. You should now work around the urn or sink, applying Polybond first then the mixture until you are satisfied with the covering. If you miss a spot, just repeat the whole process in miniature. On both pot sinks and urns cover, too, the top 5 cm (2 inches) of the *insides*. Take your scrubbing or shoe brush and pat the mixture all over to give it a rough finish before it dries – virtually rock hard within about 20–30 minutes.

in the spring and let it weather for two to three months before planting out. Although at the beginning it will not look much like genuine stone, give it time and it will: the rough texture will attract local grime, and the peat will attract algae and mosses. Look at the urn opposite. I did this a few years ago, and it has taken on that lovely, old, mature look.

If you are impatient, you can paint the covered sink or urn with a yoghurt or cow mixture as described in the *Tip*; this should speed things up. And if, at the end of a season, you are not happy with how an antiqued container has aged, you can leave it empty for the winter, the outside painted with a very cheap matt emulsion paint. This again, throughout the winter, will attract the atmosphere, algae and mosses, and will, by the time you plant it out in the spring, have taken on a lovely age.

Antiquing containers for the garden can become something of an obsessional hobby – it has with me, and my garden is full of such containers. And you don't just have to stick to urns or sinks: I have made columns or plinths from bricks or breeze blocks and they can, after a time, look very good. A pair of stone Victorian urns (the genuine articles) are now resting on a pair of such 'stone' plinths at the entrance to my garden, and they look absolutely stunning.

This urn is not stone, but plastic which has received the Bridges antiquing treatment! It's standing on a stone slab on top of a stone wall, and I have filled it with plants which are both useful and decorative – ivy, a laurel, a lovely lime-green cypress, and a hosta with, popped into the centre, a variegated leaf geranium. This gives a summer colour to the group and prevents it from looking just slightly too flat.

WOOD IN THE GARDEN

Always in search of crafty points of interest, another nice
idea is to use pieces of wood. This is not just any old
branch, but what we flower arrangers would call driftwood
– basically wood that has been 'carved' by wind, water or
some other natural means into wonderfully visual shapes.
Pieces of wood can be collected in your local wood – those
which are already green with moss are particularly attractive
– as well as by rivers or on the beach. I always think that
wood which has been seawater-sculpted has a wonderful
texture and colour, the salt presumably having an effect as
well as the action of the waves. But pieces can also be
discovered very much nearer home. I in fact unearthed
some pieces in my own garden which must have lain there
for hundreds of years: I cleaned out the holes, removing the
rotten pieces, and created some wonderful and interesting
shapes. I used one of these pieces – that in the photograph
on page 24 – in one of our national competitions a few
years ago, and some competitors from Africa wanted to
know what car sprays I had used to create the green and
mould effect on it. They couldn't believe that this was just
the result of the natural atmosphere in my part of
Yorkshire, with the mosses, lichens and algae which flourish
in the clean air there.

Another source of wood was entirely accidental. I was
motoring to Halifax a number of years ago, and an
enormous tree was being felled in the local vicarage garden.
The road had been blocked on one side and as I drove
slowly past, I could see that the tree had been eaten away in
the centre, and that pieces with wonderful internal shapes
were being piled at the side of the road. I screeched to a
halt, raced back, and asked what they were going to do

*Reared up, rather like a
modern sculpture, are
three pieces of wood
begged from a chance
encounter with a felling
team. In them,
transforming an English
country garden into
something rather more
tropical, are three ananas
(pineapple plants) –
indoor plants in the
winter. The wood pieces
have not been fixed
together, they just
beautifully balance, each
piece of the trunking
being about 30 cm (12
inches) deep, and very
heavy.*

with the wood. On being told that they would be taken to the local tip, I begged three of them, and very useful they have proved as you can see in the photograph on page 23. I cleaned them well and kept them outside for some time before using them. I also decided that I would not fix them together – as I could have done – but that I would leave them as pieces that could be used separately as decorative features in their own right, or with plants or arrangements in them.

The wood pieces can, if they're interesting enough visually, be left to stand on their own in the garden, upright or flat, as a sort of instant, do-it-yourself Moore or Hepworth modern sculpture. But I like to use them in a more crafty, flower-arranging way. In both the photographs, I have used the pieces as frameworks or bases for a garden 'flower arrangement'. This shouldn't be too elaborate or the plants too trailing, as the beauty of the shapes and textures of the wood will be hidden. I have, though, I must admit, used the vicarage pieces separately in exhibitions, with enormous flower arrangements coming out of them – to great acclaim, I might add. But, in general, the simpler the better. In both wood photographs, I have used strikingly dramatic plants – in one echeverias, in the other ananas (pineapple plants) – and in both I have created one of the basics of my crafty philosophy, a talking point, a feature of interest for the garden.

One thing you must remember, though, if you want to bring any piece of wood into your house, is to clean it thoroughly first (see page 42). Very many nasties can be lurking underneath bark and, in the case of the vicarage wood above, something had been eating away the centre of the tree. You don't want that something to start eating away at your furniture or floor boards!

Sitting on the edge of a stone wall is this lovely roundish piece of driftwood. In the summer months – because I don't want to hide the interest of the wood – I merely sit in it two lovely echeverias; in the winter I leave it empty, when it builds up its mossy surface and natural appearance.

GARDEN BACKGROUNDS

It's worth thinking briefly about these, as they can be of considerable interest in themselves. Just as pictures and ornaments look best when displayed against an uncluttered background, so too do your various points of garden interest. Walls, fences, trees or tall shrubs all provide backgrounds of varying success at the sides and back of your garden, but 'ground' backgrounds are important too.

In many cases it could be best to have an expanse of grass: a luscious green lawn is a wonderful background for the rest of the garden, just as a carpet is in a room. When I moved to my house, we discovered many York paving stones under the sods and we made large paved areas with them at first. However, we then realised it looked rather stark, so interspersed areas of gravel. This tends to give a softening effect, and also allows for ground cover plants to spring up and soften hard areas. Many people don't seem to like to see this overlapping, where plants naturally fall and flow over paved areas, thinking it untidy. I think it's natural.

I also think the contrast of *textures* is interesting: my chimney pot collection, for instance, is displayed against York stone paving, but with gravel interspersed. Again this softens what could be a very hard area. The troughs, too, are displayed against areas of sea-washed pebbles: I water them with the sprinkler, and wet, they look wonderful. Sand could get carried to other parts of the garden, but in the odd space you could recreate that feeling of Japanese tranquillity by raking it decoratively, and perhaps 'lifting' it with some driftwood or stones, in a 'collage'. Always, with your focal points, try to site them against backgrounds which are equally as interesting.

There might be room somewhere for a 'collage' of driftwood pieces and stones which could be arranged against an interesting garden background – perhaps York stone or other surface, against a plain wall or, as here, on an area of raked sand, rather à la japonaise.

'Instant' gardening in the form of baskets and plants with a garden 'collage' of brooms. I attached the brooms first of all to the ivied wall, before attaching two of the baskets. The greens in the baskets are the prime interest — here lots of good old traditional ivies — and then I added lots of seasonal and complementary coloured flowers (in their pots) : geraniums, begonias, pelargoniums and hydrangeas. A wonderful focal point for any garden — and think how effective it would look in blues and whites with the touches of lime green.

'INSTANT' GARDENING

For a sort of 'instant' gardening, and again to create focal points, you could have windowboxes full of decorative and useful plants. These can create an all-year-round interest if you plan them (those wonderful boxes outside London banks, building societies and hotels could give you some ideas), but I often have boxes that are all green. During the winter months they have ivies, very slow-growing cypress and my favourite plant of this type, the spotted laurel, which has its foliage for 12 months of the year. (As a flower arranger, you can keep its size well under control.) In late spring, early summer, up pops my dear old hosta, and throughout the whole summer my boxes are full of a variety of greens which are most attractive. You could, of course, introduce seasonal colour as with some of the containers already mentioned: bulbs in the spring, or polyanthus; geraniums and chrysanthemums in the summer and autumn respectively. I have often used a less usual plant, the kalanchoe. It's an indoor plant basically, which used to come only in orange, but is now available in reds, pinks and creams. I saw them on a demonstration visit to the West Indies as an outdoor plant, and wondered whether they would work for us at home. We first tried them a couple of summers ago, and in my boxes and urns they flower magnificently for the whole of the summer, and give tremendous value for money.

Hanging baskets could have the same sort of treatment, using all green plants, or adding relevant colour in the various seasons. Use moss and peat or, an interesting idea that has recently been developed, those linings of compressed peat which look like an old ARP warden's helmet. These can be pushed into any shape of basket as they're quite flexible, but they mustn't actually be broken; they retain moisture well and keep the plants looking very healthy.

Other sorts of baskets could be used to form a focal point against a wall or background, fixed or standing on a table. I do this occasionally in my own garden, as in the photograph on pages 28-9, and fill the baskets with plants (see the *Tip* below).

T   I   P

For an instant basket of colourful glory, buy baskets from your local garden centre, store or junk shop – old shopping baskets from the 1940s are still cheap to buy and have a good shape (willow weathers well). Line them with polythene, stapling or wiring it in place at the top. Put a couple of handfuls of peat in the bottom to retain moisture, and stand a *potted* plant – or two, or three – on top.

A final idea for a focal point could be a sort of garden collage, this time on a wall. When clearing out your garden shed, you may come across some old gardening implements which aren't usable – an old cracked spade or broken rake, a tatty sieve or an old watering can with a hole in it. If you've got a blank wall which nothing can grow against, you could put masonry nails in at various intervals, paint the implements white (or leave them as they are, with wood texture and rust showing), and hang them in an interesting configuration. They could be hooked down at the end of each season, repainted and regrouped in a different way next year. Another simple but unusual focal point for your crafty flower arranger's garden, which, with all the others in the previous pages, demonstrates just how far you are able to stray from the conventional lobelia and alyssum borders!

Chapter Two

The Crafty Collector

(Previous page) I'm sure the reaction of many of you to the picture of me in my glory-hole loft with some of my collected treasures will be, 'What a load of old rubbish'! In one sense, yes, but I know what's there, where exactly it is, and that I'll find a use for that wicker base, that figurine, that glass dome or those date palm fronds at some time or another.

I don't think that I have to tell any flower arranger about collecting: it's one of the first passions, and you just cannot *be* a flower arranger without a multitude of bits and pieces. You only have to visit a flower show or two and see what those 'crafty' folk get up to, to understand what I mean. Everyone starts off at the beginning with the simple 'vases', but then the bug gets them to produce something that is more out of the ordinary; particularly when you start entering flower shows, you want something that is quite different from that used by the arranger in the next niche.

It is a question of training your eyes, and you mustn't blink too much, you might miss something! It's difficult for me to say where to look and what to look for, because possibilities just *abound*. You would be amazed at where I have picked up objects that have been made up into flower-arranging accessories or containers, and it's not very often that I am left empty-handed. Perhaps, on one of my many visits to Spain, I may have been rather upset that a broken piece of stone balustrading from a balcony could not be brought home – still, next time, who knows!

For Free

There are many things that are collectable that cost nothing at all. Driftwood readily comes to mind, and I've already discussed its use in the garden. The only problem is finding a beach or river bank that has not already been plundered by other crafty flower arrangers. It doesn't stop there though: shells, stones, mosses, bark and seed heads are collectable and useful too. And for those who are fortunate enough to go abroad – especially to the tropical areas of the world – there are glorious treasures to be found.

For a Few Pence

Apart from 'nature' finds, junk and charity shops are good hunting grounds for flower-arranging containers and accessories, and it doesn't matter if there's a chip in the edge or it's the wrong colour. I look out in markets, junk stalls and such places for the things that everyone else passes by, but don't forget I have been training my eye for many years. That black lacquered base, once holding a bowling club trophy, was it 10p? With a curvy table or chair leg mounted on to it, and a slightly rusty jelly mould on top, all screwed, glued and spray-painted, this 'new' container could win you best in show next time. In Chapter Three, where I describe how to make crafty containers from crafty collectables, you'll see what I mean.

Get to know your local plumber, joiner and, best of all, your local stone and monumental mason. Those wonderful offcuts of marble tombstone are fantastic for bases, and for a few pence he'll be happy to see you again. I cultivate a few of these chaps, and it's 'Just give us a few flowers for the missus'.

Another vital aspect of crafty collecting is the space in which to store all your bits and pieces. I'm lucky in that I have enormous lofts, and with a loft ladder and some good lighting, I've got my own glory hole in which to store and work to my heart's content. I've also got everything arranged in a neat and orderly fashion – catalogued in labelled boxes – which makes finding some particular item easy. I think this is very important, as there's nothing worse than knowing you have something but not being able to find it when you want it.

So, happy hunting, and I hope I don't see too many of you in *my* hunting grounds.

'NATURE' FINDS

I would imagine that every flower arranger has, at some time and in some part of the world, combed a beach, river bank or wood looking for something interesting that can be used in their art. As your flower-arranging 'eye' develops, you will almost immediately recognise the potential of a variety of things: when you're starting, you may not realise that something quite unlikely could so easily have a change of use, and contribute enormously to the simplest arrangement. In one way, *being* a flower arranger gives you a sense of useful purpose: whether child or adult, we all pick up natural things such as stones and shells, admiring their beauty and wanting to keep them. As a flower arranger you can actually *use* them, avoiding thereto possible later relegation to the back of a cupboard, or the dustbin.

However, to be a proper crafty collector, you need to be organised. I've said this many times before, but you must never set out on any collecting expedition without one or more plastic bags. If you're strolling along a beach in some sunny clime, for instance, there won't be much room in your minute bikini to store shells or corals – a plastic bag is the answer. And when you're travelling abroad, take a box in which to bring treasures home. Go to your local flower shop and ask if you can have a medium-sized flower box, with lid and base, which will fold flat. This goes into the bottom of your suitcase.

If you don't find anything worthwhile – but that's unlikely – you can just discard the box or bring it back with you. If you do find some treasures – fan corals, dried seed pods or palm leaves, lovely bracts and spathes from the palm trees, dried gourds – you can pack them carefully in the box, tie it up with string (take that with you too, string is quite difficult to find in some parts of the world), and then send it through with your luggage. When you arrive at your home destination, just go through the red channel and say you're a flower arranger – I say I'm a demonstrator of flower arranging. If they want to have a look (for some items are not allowed – things on the root for example), you can simply open the box rather than try to rummage through the next fortnight's washing! To be a successful collector, you must emulate the boy scout or girl guide you once were, and be prepared!

A typical Bridges return from abroad – here from the West Indies – a small suitcase and larger flower box full of finds: dried seed heads and palmetto palm leaves, the odd fan I was given, and wood roses. The gourds with the ends cut off are used there hung from trees with a lamp inside for barbecue parties: I've since used them very successfully in arrangements. There are also a few stand-by items I took out with me for my demonstrations.

Arranging Exotic Finds

Having brought back your wonderful bits and pieces, the first thing you will want to do as a flower arranger is to arrange them. I too like to use them straightaway, but I don't think they want to be lived with permanently. I always think of dried or preserved materials as standby material for when flowers are too costly, not available or when the weather is bad. You can use them in an arrangement, enjoy them in all their exotic glory, then, after a while you can dismantle it and store the items carefully again. Having been on many trips over the last few years, my collection is becoming very big, but even stuff brought back from visits some 20 years ago is still with me, still usable and still used.

With some of these treasures from home and foreign collecting, I like to do arrangements such as the one opposite – virtually a round-the-world arrangement as I've used material from the West Indies, Australia, Africa and Europe. I love this natural wood look, with its interesting textures and varieties, and so I matched the container and indeed the background to the materials I was using. Some people dislike dried materials, referring to them as dead-looking, but I think they're wonderful in all their variety – to me it's what Mother Nature's flower arranging is all about. The container is very much home-made – from junk items I've craftily collected (see pages 46 and 64) – and the pressed flower picture, although 15 years old, looks as good today as it did originally (see page 101). I could happily live with this arrangement for quite some while, and every time I look at it I'm reminded – one of the major advantages of being a crafty collector – of a wonderful holiday or trip: the items are beautiful mementoes of countries, places, even individual gardens, where I have been relaxed and happy.

In a very much home-made container (see page 64), I've arranged some of my exotic foreign finds: lovely cone shapes, wood roses, curving pods, trembling grass seed heads, with leaves and whirls of cane to give movement. It needed a little weight at the bottom, so I placed a second little arrangement on the marble base at the foot of the container.

Collecting from Beaches and River Banks

Shells are the 'nature' finds most associated with serious study and collection, and, although there are some interesting varieties to be found in the UK and on the Continent, the best come from beaches further afield – from the Pacific, the Caribbean, and those wonderful shell beaches of Florida, on the Gulf of Mexico. Collections of shells can be used in a variety of ways: simply arranged on a bathroom shelf to show off all their fascinating shapes and colours, or in a dome or glass jar; as accessories in arrangements (see page 133); actually *holding* arrangements; or in a collage as opposite. But they must be cleaned thoroughly first (see the *Tip* overleaf).

Turn first to Chapter Four for more detail about collage making, and how to set about making bases etc., before embarking on something like the collage opposite. You can see very clearly the tremendous variety of textures, shapes and forms you can achieve with your collected shells and corals. The backing here is solid wood – the shells weigh a lot – covered with raw silk wall covering, and the first placements were those lovely lacy sea fern corals. They were glued on with ordinary glue, as were some of the smaller shells. For the heavier shells I had to use epoxy resin glue – where you mix two compounds together – and I must recommend that you use these glues in very small amounts, as some set solidly before you've time to make your placements.

As the collage materials were so heavy and bulky – the brain coral at the front stands almost 6 cm (2½ inches) off the surface – I used little cardboard rolls to wedge them in place while the glue set. Then, once I built up the main group, where the larger shells are, I went back and put on a further level of a smaller shell here or lace coral there. But

When this shell collage was finished it must have weighed about 6.75 kg (15 lb), so you can appreciate why I needed a strong backing board and strong glue! The whole has a wonderful 3-D effect, with the brown of the scallop shell backs and the blue of the peacock's ears echoing the colours of the tropical seas where they originated.

T I P

Some conchologist friends in Mombasa told me how to
get rid of that shell smell – and I think you will know
what I mean by 'that smell'! All you do is put some
paraffin in a bucket and stand the shells in it for about a
week. Take them out, hose or swill them down with
water, and 'that smell' (as well as any hidden life forms)
will have disappeared. Simply dry the shells and then
polish them with a soft cloth. They'll look magnificent.

---

don't over-do it and spoil it.

I didn't frame the collage as I wanted it to look like a
panel in my downstairs bathroom, but it *could* be framed.
It's a very simple process, and I tell you how to do it on
page 86.

Driftwood too can be picked up on river banks and
beaches and I've already talked about its possibilities in the
garden. However, before bringing it into the house, you
must give it a little treatment to get rid of any bugs that
may be in it. Sea water usually kills most things, but you
want to be sure. Swill and scrub it down with a bleach and
water mix, and then dry thoroughly. (Don't over-bleach, or
it can look artificial.) The thing I like most about driftwood
is that it comes in so many varieties, textures and surfaces:
that from the Caribbean is a lovely blonde; that from
Scotland is grey and very old looking; other pieces are
covered with wonderful mosses and algae.

Stones, large and small, can be collected too from
beaches and river banks, and you can see in the garden
'collage' on page 27 one way of using them. They too, like
shells, speak of their origins – basalt from here, granite
from there, quartz, flint, limestone and sandstone (perhaps
with fossil remnants), and slices of slate. They come in a
variety of colours and shapes, some smoothed by the action

*A moss river bank,
magnificent in its natural
state. Take just a little; it
will keep damp in a
polythene bag for months
and will be very useful in
simple line arrangements
to disguise the pinholder
and mechanics.*

of wind and water, some jagged and dramatic, and all have wonderful decorative qualities.

I find stones very useful. Not only do they look good just placed among pebble patches in the garden, or in water in glass jars, but they're particularly valuable in landscape type arrangements: a few pebbles on a piece of slate, with some moss, a nice piece of wood and a few flowers can make a very natural looking arrangement. But keep these *simple* – like the one in the photograph opposite – because if you put everything but the kitchen sink in, they'll lose their point. And if you wonder who on earth would do an arrangement on a river bank – with reference to that next photograph – think about the stream running through your garden, or your nice pond or pool with a rock formation next to it. For flower arranging *can* be done outside too. I once helped at a Yorkshire flower festival where shapes of polystyrene holding flower arrangements were floated in the swimming pool: a wonderful idea and it was talked about for weeks afterwards. I've seen an old wheelbarrow outside someone's house which was filled with a new flower arrangement every week, and I always have a small arrangement on my patio table during the summer for when we sit out. Your flower arranging should *not* stop at the front door.

When collecting from river banks and woods, try not to spoil the environment. The odd little piece of moss or stone isn't going to make all that much difference, but the countryside will definitely suffer if you're greedy and go along with your estate car, masses of bags and boxes, and denude a moss or pebble river bank.

Here, by the flowing river, I have arranged a simple branch and five daffodils brought from my own garden, in a container holding a pinholder and some moss. The stones at the bottom finish off a very natural looking group.

JUNK FINDS

The finds so far have been for free, from nature, but the collecting goes on and on, a never-ending process. Some junk can be picked up for nothing – the throw-outs on the local tip – or for a few pence in junk or charity shops, jumble or car-boot sales. Occasionally something that is a bit damaged can be picked up fairly cheaply in an antique shop. For the objects or items for use in flower arranging, whether as containers or accessories, don't need to be perfect, as I keep saying: the odd chip can be covered with an element of your arrangement, and cracks and unpleasing colours can be disguised by paint, 'antiquing' (see page 72), or other process. You have to develop the eye for all these things, as many wouldn't seem immediately to have much flower-arranging potential. Have a look at the next few pages, and I think you'll see what I mean.

As an example, look at the wooden container on page 39, which holds natural collected items. The 'stem' is the leg of what must have been a magnificent boardroom table; this had obviously been broken up and the pieces were bound for the local tip. The four legs were sticking up like a wooden Stonehenge, so I acquired them (three of which are in the photograph on page 65). One was for the container I mention above, one became the leg of a rather nice side table. The base plate and container top were found, years later, in a flea market in Paris. With a little glueing, screwing and ingenuity, I combined them all for a very useful container, the making of which I describe on page 64. The potential of junk indeed!

You may collect particular items, which will have a use in flower-arranging. I, for instance, have collected glass for many years and you can see some of the items in the photograph below. Hardly any of them started off as containers for use with flowers, but I have adapted them: if it will hold a pinholder or floral foam, as I always say, it will hold a flower arrangement. Just take a quick look in your local junk shop and you will see what tremendous scope there is in glass objects – sugar bowls, milk jugs, dessert bowls and that wonderful Irish crystal container at the top here, given to me as a gift. Cake stands are a particular favourite of mine, and you can see in the following pages how I use them as a container for a fantastic arrangement.

Cake Stands

The great beauty of these cake stands is their variety of size and design. They reigned supreme over tea tables from Edwardian times up to the 1940s, and just decades later were relegated to church bazaars and jumble sales. I must now have about 30 of every shape and size, and I don't just use them for flowers: we have one – a set of seven – on a worktop in our kitchen holding the week's supply of fruit and vegetables, a pyramid of ever-changing colour; another is in the bathroom, holding a collection of holiday souvenir soaps.

A selection from my glass collection. Even just arranged like this, glass can look interesting!

1. The container used here is a selection of differently sized individual cake stands, bowls and dishes, all on top of each other. The bottom dish sits on a piece of round glass mirror to add that interesting reflection to the arrangement. A piece of soaked floral foam is attached to the stem of each cake stand with wire and a piece is placed in the middle of the sugar bowl at the top. Work all the areas in unison, so that you get this wonderful, flowing waterfall effect from one level of the arrangement to the next. I've used various foliages from the garden, as well as some from a kentia or howeia palm (a house plant) which

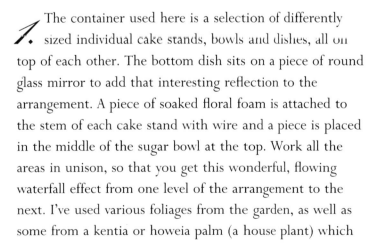

gives those lovely delicate finger shapes to the sides. The slender curves are pampas grass foliage, and variegated *canariensis* ivy creates the knots of heavier foliage at the centre of each arrangement.

2. Once the foliage has created the basic shape, height and width of the arrangement, the flowers can start to be added. As I have a great passion for green and white, particularly with glass, I used some gypsophila (Bristol fairy) and September flowers (mini michaelmas daisies) to give a very fine delicate outline. Coming in towards the centre part of the arrangements – and *still* work all four together – I've got buds of spray carnations.

3. As the focal point of each level I used the open flowers of spray carnations and 'Bonnie Jean' spray chrysanthemums. (These latter are available all year round, and I find them extraordinarily useful.) With the arrangement complete, you can see how handy these cake stands can be, and you can still see the beauty of the glass itself at the various levels. This could be placed with its back to the wall on a hall table or in the centre of a buffet table, bringing the cake stands back to a former glory, but in a totally different way.

Victorian Glass Domes

For years I've also collected the glass domes used in
Victorian times to cover clocks, stuffed birds and animals,
or wax fruit. I use the domes and their bases for a number
of display purposes – for arrangements of dried flowers or,
as on page 97, for antique hatpins from my wife Pat's huge
collection. Domes are still to be found but they're now
rather expensive, I'm afraid.

In this small dome – only about 21 cm (8½ inches) high
– I wanted to surround my oriental porcelain goddess figure
with a garden of 'porcelain' flowers. To find flower shapes
and sizes that wouldn't overpower her, I searched through
the catalogued boxes in my loft. There I unearthed some
flowers from a Victorian headdress, some lace Maltese ones,
and some plastic flowers, leaves and fern shapes. The latter
were dipped into white gloss paint to give them their
porcelain look. A wire stem was attached to each and made
into a hook at the free end. The flower was dipped and
then hung from the hook on a garden cane between two
chairs over a piece of paper to drip dry. I did this four
times on each flower before I was really satisfied – it took
me about a week in all to prepare, before I started work on
the actual group.

I glued the figure down on to the velvet base of the
dome then fixed a large knob of plasticine at the back to
take the flowers. I started at the top and created sweeping
lines round, bringing the main weight of the flowers
flowing down towards the front. Every 10 minutes or so, I
looked at the group from the back as well, and kept lifting
the dome on: it's amazing how the look of one of these
arrangements alters completely once the dome is in place.
And it mustn't ever become too squashed looking – a fault
of the Victorians themselves.

A grouping of goddess and
plant shapes underneath a
small glass dome.
Although it all looks as
though made from the
finest porcelain, only the
goddess is – the rest is
'crafty'!

Kitchen and Household Collectables

These are great favourites with my family as we're so interested in food and cooking, and I've used a collection of old implements in the wall arrangement on page 140. Here, however, I've utilised some of my flatiron collection, an old steam iron, and the family coffee grinder, to create an arrangement in the kitchen.

On a base that would once have held a Victorian clock, I placed a kettle trivet to hold up the steam iron with, at the opposite end, the coffee grinder. The interior of the steam iron holds the drifoam for the major part of the arrangement, and the open grinder drawer the foam for the second part. At the back and sides I supported some small flatirons, those used for collars and cuffs.

As I wanted something slightly permanent and woody looking to match the units, everything is natural except for some sprays of a lovely bronze silk fern. Rhythm and movement at the top are brought in by fine cane drawn along the back of a knife for whirl shapes. To the middle are seed pods, cones, poppy heads, a wood rose, leaf shapes cut from one large leaf, and dried gourds and pomegranates. The ring shapes used top and bottom are minute willow rings.

Using a steam iron called Edna, several flatirons, and a coffee grinder, I've created an arrangement for the kitchen with dried and preserved materials and, courtesy of my flower arranger's licence, a piece of silk fern. I've also used these accessories in other arrangements, with foliage, fruit and vegetables, and with cottage garden and wild flowers. They all look interesting.

T I P

When drying pomegranates, be patient. They're very fleshy, so there's a lot to dry. I dry them simply in my fruit bowl, where they contribute their shape and colour during the process, but this can take *up to 12 months*. Don't bruise or puncture them or they'll rot, but during this drying time they'll acquire an old leather look, and they'll be amazingly useful in all your dried arrangements.

Weaving Shuttles

For a final example of what can be done with junk items,
I've used weaving shuttles which are quite commonly
available in the north. They're usually just there for the
taking before being thrown on the nearest bonfire as, with
the demise of so much of the textile industry in the north,
many mills have closed down. There are a few mills still
operational – two in Hebden Bridge near me, and some still
going strong in Huddersfield – but even there the shuttles
get worn as they ply to and fro on the frames, and are
replaced by new ones. So they're around and, although you
may never have considered it, can be used as very effective
containers for flower arrangements.

These arrangements here are really to show you how the
shuttles can be used – lying flat *or* fixed to or hanging on
the wall. The hanks of wool on the spindles are just for
show in a sense – although the shapes are good, as are the
colours and textures. (Knitting shops are almost as
colourful as flower shops, with their rainbows of balls and
hanks on display.)

As you can see, there is an opening in the shuttle, and
drifoam can be fixed there to take the dried materials. Fix
in with floral foam tape, and don't use items that are too
large or over-size. As in all dried flower arrangements,
always have a planned colour scheme – using, as here, all
creams, yellows and oranges, autumnal colours – rather
than mixing colours rather more haphazardly. Everything
should tone with and complement everything else.

In all these preceding pages, I hope I've shown you how
to develop your crafty collector's 'eye', how to look at
objects with your art in mind, and see potential in even the
most unlikely things. Happy hunting.

*My 'collected' containers
here are weaving shuttles,
and the materials used are
dried: there is dried corn,
fern shapes, cones, beech
nut husks, whirls of cord
and pipecleaners as well
as fruit shapes, lacquered
to look like wood –
anything to give texture,
variety and interest. Both
arrangements are finished
off with a bow of natural
hessian ribbon.*

Chapter Three

CRAFTY CONTAINERS

*W*hat *are* containers? We flower arrangers know that they're what we put our flower arrangements into. They're not the vases (vorzes, vaizes) or bowls commercially produced for flower arranging – these to me are simply receptacles for holding flowers. Here, although we've already seen many quite different ideas for containers, I'm going to describe how you can make or adapt your own. And why should you want to do this? Simply because it's always the unusual, the one-off that we flower arrangers want. Some things – the tincrafting for instance – are described in detail; other things can't be as detailed because I can only give you the *idea* – it's unlikely that you'll be able to acquire exactly the same bits and pieces as I've used.

Containers from Throw-outs

And once again, as always, the ideas will utilise to a large extent everyone else's throw-outs. I don't actually think there's anything that has been thrown out that I can't do something with, and the local tip and junk shops are absolute gold-mines for me. What other people don't value any more I leap upon with enthusiasm – although I must admit the men at the tip do eye me a little suspiciously from time to time!

Let me give you one idea for a start. Empty baked bean tins. The first time I used these was as lifts – washed, brushed up and covered with fabric – but now they're the basis of my tincrafting ideas for flower-arranging containers and accessories. Plastic containers – water and washing-up liquid bottles – can be transformed into useful items as well: when in Spain I have made flower containers and fruit bowls from the large water bottles there, left plain or unpainted. Think too of how you will be helping the world refuse-disposal problems by utilising empty tins or plastic

I hope that you will study the photograph on the previous page, and – once you know what some of the crafty basics for the containers are – that it will set your minds tingling with possibilities. The column is plumbers' fall pipe; the goblets were originally nasty plastic; the lifts are biscuit tins; one candleholder, the peacock and star are made from baked bean tins; and the hanging container is a washing-up liquid container! The collages, as well as several other pieces, have been created using humble pasta shapes and string.

bottles, instead of throwing them away!

Another idea involves a little more skill – firstly, the 'eye' to see potential in a table leg and some round pieces of metal, and secondly, the ability to bring them all together into something useful. If you read how I did it, you should, I hope, be inspired to collect and make something similar for yourselves.

Adapting Containers

As I have said, *any*thing – or virtually anything – can be made into a container, and even if it doesn't look too promising at first you can always transform it by some crafty camouflage – at its simplest, spray-painting. A junk-shop find of a ghastly colour can always be painted, but 'antiquing' some containers gives them a complete new lease of life – and it involves little more than a couple of coats of spray paint and a little 'hand work'. (This, please note, is a different type of antiquing to that described in Chapter One!)

Some simple modern containers can be made by adding textures and surface to bought or junk objects. These additions could be more traditional lace or paper shapes, or they could be objects I expect many of you won't ever have considered in relation to container making or flower arranging. I, in fact, used string, pasta and sugar lumps! (Where does he get these ideas from, I hear you ask.)

There really is no limit to what you can do, given the will, the way and the 'eye'. I hope that the containers and various other crafty ideas in the following pages will set your imagination working.

TINCRAFTING

This is something I started many years ago, and I just love the idea of making something from literally nothing. For the basic ingredient is old food tins – yes, baked bean and other tins, washed, labels removed and then transformed. Once you start, you will be constantly amazed at the many applications and combinations that you will end up with – the candleholder, flower or star and peacock I show here are only the tip of the tincrafting possibilities – and each project will lead you on to another.

The prime object, of course, is to create something that is fun to do, and that will be fun to possess afterwards, something that you can use as a flower-arranging container or accessory. It doesn't require much artistic skill – more manual dexterity – nor do you need particularly expensive tools. One, in fact, will already be in your kitchen drawer. As you need to remove the top rim of the tin before you can cut the metal, I would recommend that you use (or acquire) one of those screw-action tin openers which take lid *and* rim off cleanly in one go. This will save you time and aching wrists trying to cut the rim off with your cutters. I actually use tinsmith's snips which are not expensive, and are available from DIY shops and especially designed for the job. The third tool is a pair of very fine-nose pincers: I think these are the sort normally used by electricians, and again they're not expensive.

Once the top rim of the tin is removed with the tin opener, you are left with a straight-sided canister with base, the start of any form of tincrafting. Now, using your tinsmith's snips, cut the sides of the can into approximately 2 cm (¾ inch) even sections from the rimless top down to the base, starting at the seam. There will be 11 to 12, ending up at the seam – which you cut away for a candleholder, star or flower, and retain for a peacock.

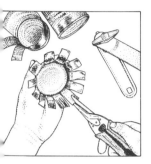

1. Now cut each of these sections down into five little thin strips as here – virtually to the bottom for a candleholder, a third of the way down for a star, flower or peacock. Keep the sections of metal straight up for a candleholder, folded out as here for a star, flower or peacock.

2. Once you've cut all the sections into strips (I've only done a few here), take each little piece of metal strip separately into the pincers at the very end and squeeze. Roll the metal over the nose of the pincers, pull the pincers out, and you have made a lovely curl. Do this curling on all the strips – in or out, as you please – almost to the bottom and evenly for the candleholder; make them of varying lengths, coming to a point, for the flower, star or peacock.

Candleholder

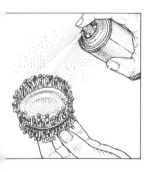

3. Make two of these cut and evenly rolled tins and glue their solid bases together with epoxy resin (the only glue that will work with metal), curls facing outwards. When dry and fixed, gild with spray paint. The holder stands on one set of curls, the fat candle (it's always difficult to find suitable holders for them) is held in the other.

Star or Flower

4. These, too, are made from two completely cut and
rolled tins, but the second tin is glued into the *inside*
of the first, the 'petals' of both curling out at angles. You
could, in fact, if you get enough tin sizes, do up to five
layers of petals. Gild as for the candleholder.

The seam held in the pincers here is removed for a star
or flower, but it is vital for the peacock, the basis of which
is this star or flower shape.

Peacock

5. Cut both top and base off a third tin and cut
through along the seam to make a long flat piece of
metal. Cut off the seam, and retain as a 'leg'. Draw a body,
beak and plumed head shape on the metal piece, and cut
out. Cut down the 'plume' part into strips and roll as in 1
and 2.

6. Now glue all the various bits together. Use one of
the tin lids as a base and glue the seam 'legs' to it,
along with the body. Gild with spray paint when firm and
add something interesting to the middle of the body part if
you like – here a Christmas decoration with some glitter
dusted over the top.

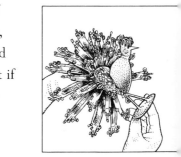

In the photograph here, you can see the tincrafting
results in more detail. A couple of such candleholders
would grace any dining table, and I don't think anybody
could say they look like baked bean tins! Likewise the star
or flower which, hanging above a gilded mirror with a
ribbon bow suspended from it, would defy its humble
origins. And a pair of peacocks would look fantastic at
Christmas, either side of a gilded centrepiece.

The hanging piece I'll tell you about in the next section.

OTHER CRAFTY JUNK
CONVERSIONS

Apart from tins – probably the ultimate junk – you could also use plastic bottles, and the hanging object in the previous photograph is a washing-up liquid container. I cut slits into the sides to make it look like an open-work cage, then gilded it. A metal ring screw was fixed securely on the top to make a hanger. The plant material is a lovely piece of contorted hazel, also gilded, with little leaf and metal flower shapes glued on. A few of these hanging together would look wonderful at Christmas, and imagine it in a slightly larger version holding holly, artificial poinsettias and a ribbon bow.

But now for one of my favourite containers, using that forlorn table leg talked about on page 46, and illustrated with an arrangement in it on page 39. This is truly an amalgam of crafty collecting and crafty combining for a container (as is another container, illustrated on page 141).

1. Here (right) are three of the boardroom table legs I found in a skip; one as it was originally, dusty and dirty; the second cut down to take a side-table top; and the third polished to make this container. Around them are displayed the other container-making ingredients – the bowl top and base (a metal ceiling rose?) picked up from a wonderful stall in the Paris flea market – as were all the other bits and pieces. (I'll find a use for *them* some day soon.)

2. The metal bowl top with its convenient hole in the centre, was fixed to the top of the leg with a long screw and washer, and likewise the round base part was screwed on from underneath. As I didn't want it to *look* like

an old table leg with bits of metal added top and bottom, I
needed something to bring the two metal areas together
and hit upon those strips.

3. I'm sure I could have found metal strips in Paris, but
these are plastic, the stuff sold in DIY shops to stick
on wardrobe fronts (they're useful too in collages, see page
79). I gilded these, 'antiqued' them a little (see page 72),
and glued them in place on the fluted part of the leg.

APPLICATION FOR TRANSFORMATION

No, I'm not suggesting that you yourself need application to transform objects into crafty containers (although it helps). It's imagination and vision that you need, rather, and the application is of objects to *other* objects. You've just encountered this in the table leg container overleaf, and in the photograph on pages 56–7 you'll see a large selection of what I mean. At its simplest, the 'lift' to the left of the picture is a lidless biscuit tin with a velvet and braid application. The goblet on top is plastic, cheap to buy and very uninteresting: lace flower and leaf motifs were glued on to the bowl and foot, and old lampshade braid around the top, before the whole was gilded. The other goblet is plastic too, spray-painted black – as was its biscuit tin lift – and then on to both were glued cut-outs from silver doilies.

However the other application ideas, if no less simple in concept, are much more crafty.

Glass and Sugar Lumps

The idea for this 'application' came quite by accident when I spilled some sugar lumps on to a piece of mirror at my shop. The container itself, although it looks black, is made from pieces of mirror tiles with bevelled edges. These were glued together with epoxy resin to form the square shape. (To hold it together while drying I sticky-taped down the joins and packed crumpled newspaper inside.) It sits on another mirror tile.

At one side of the container I created a Christmas tree shape with the cubes of sugar. I glued on the first layer, then gave it a 3-D effect by glueing some more levels into the centre of the tree. I thought the base looked a bit bare,

so I glued some more sugar on to the mirror to look like
the shadow of the tree.

All it needed then was a very simple arrangement. A
piece of drifoam inside, and a dead hawthorn branch with
all its knobbly bits on to which you can glue some little
flowers. I give lots of hints about these 'bonsai' trees and
blossoms later, but the blooms here are cut from three
sprays of those clear plastic flowers which, in certain lights,
gleam like spilled petrol. A final addition of three frosted
sprays of fern and some glass baubles, and a Christmas
arrangement is complete.

> *T I P*
> If you wanted to use this mirror-tile container for fresh
> flowers, wedge a small plastic container inside to take
> the soaked floral foam. The container is solid enough,
> but it's *not* waterproof!

*The container here is
hand-made from mirror
tiles glued together, but
the 'application' which
has transformed it is sugar
lumps!*

String and Cord

Go into any hardware shop, and you will see the huge
variety of string and cord types available, all of which I use
for container conversions and indeed for collages as here.
For the greatest interest, you need a selection of thicknesses
just as you would need a selection of flower shapes in an
arrangement. Some strings you buy in the ball, others – the
thicker sorts – you can buy by the metre.

This container I bought already covered in some rattan
or fine basketwork. I thought it lacked interest, so I added
some whirl and curl washing-line shapes around the sides.
These were glued on after a pencil marking of the shape,
and held in place with some hammered-in pins – the line is
heavy and tends to move – until the glue dried. To hide the
frayed ends I used some nut-shell flowers – the shells of
pistachio nuts glued into a flower shape with a bead in the
middle. These could also be used for the 'bonsai' tree idea
in Chapter Six: glue the flower shape on to a tiny piece of
card, cut the visible card away and then glue on to the
branches. The arrangement in the container is of curled
cane, dried seed heads and leaves.

Before attempting the collage, do please turn to Chapter
Four for details about the whole skill of collage making.
This collage was built up on hardboard covered with rough
hessian. The design was marked with pencil, and the main
S is of washing line, glued on as above. With thinner strings
and cords – even shoelaces – I created round, leaf, whirl
and triangular shapes.

The collage was originally in tones of cream, but I gilded
it with spray paint. Any time you want a change, you could
spray-paint it a different colour – the textures and varieties
of the strings and cords will always make it look interesting.

*String is very interesting
to look at with its various
thicknesses, textures and
colours, and I've used it
here to transform a
container in a very simple
fashion, and to make a
swirling collage.*

For this fat candleholder, I used a cheap double-height plastic container for flower arranging, and glued on – in sections – the first layer of pasta shapes – these are called penne *or quills. This was left to dry well before the second layer, of* ruote, *or wheels, was glued on. The whole thing was then gilded, like the finished container in the photograph.*

Pasta

There are many intriguing shapes of pasta – thin and thick lengths, spirals, rings, butterflies, shells and bows among them – and I've used them in a variety of ways. One of my favourite ideas is to apply them to containers, making them look like pieces by Stuart Devlin, an Australian goldsmith whose work I greatly admire. He makes goblets and containers which are encrusted in the same way – but with the real thing – and they're fantastic.

A pasta collage picture can be very interesting (see the photograph of mine on pages 56–7), and it's a cheap way of keeping the children quiet during the school holidays! (Crafty Derek meets Blue Peter, if you like, and again, see Chapter Four for more details about making collage pictures.) I used a hardboard backing, rough side up, to give texture and a good surface for the pasta to adhere to. The design is very modern and 3-D – the middle group stands almost 4 cm (1¾ inches) off the backing. I painted it all white, with matt paint, but it took me *ages* and at least three cans of paint. However, with that painstaking basis, it only takes a few squirts of white spray paint to bring it back to its original brightness. (It's one of their few disadvantages, but collages like these tend to collect a lot of dust.)

Another use of pasta collage work is around a picture frame. There isn't room to illustrate this, but basically, on an old plain frame that had lost its lustre, I did a collage completely round the outside of the frame – working with all the lovely whirls, curls, shells and wheels, and glueing them on in layers as I've done for the containers opposite. When it was gilded it looked wonderful, and with a Christmas type collage in the middle, for instance, it would make a very interesting wall decoration.

The basis of this modern-looking container – inspired by Stuart Devlin's work – is a piece of plumbers' plastic fall pipe, a material which I've often used: as a column (see pages 56–7), or 'antiqued' with Polybond and sand as for the garden (see page 18), often with a rope or string application as well. It's very useful stuff. Here, I simply glued on a few layers of pasta – penne and ruote *again – and then gilded the lot. A small plastic container in the top holds the drifoam, candles, sprayed lotus seed pods and whirls of cane.*

'ANTIQUING' CONTAINERS

This too is an idea which I've worked on for a number of years – and it's quite different from the antiquing of *garden* containers. As I'm always saying, the crafty flower arranger should always keep his or her eyes open for something that has possibilities. He or she must look in shops and stores for containers that have *shape*: the colour or look may be ghastly, but if the *shape* is good, then something can be done with it. Whether the container or accessory is plaster, metal, wood or plastic, it can be 'antiqued' to make it look very much more interesting. It could be a plaster lamp-base, a cherub shape which has been painted badly, or indeed a statuette or figure which isn't in very good condition (turn to page 141 to see how I 'antiqued' one of these after repairing).

The first requisite though is a marked or moulded surface. If you look at the goblets on pages 56–7, they had no surface until I applied lace or doily pieces. You need some relief on to which to 'antique' successfully. Also on that page is a column, very useful for flower arrangers. This is a piece of plumbers' fall pipe again, to which I applied pieces of half-round wood dowelling and some plastic wardrobe moulding (as for the table leg container on page 65). This too has been 'antiqued' as opposite, and I don't think anyone would ever guess at its humble sanitary origins!

The ingredients needed for 'antiquing' are really very few: gold spray paint, black spray paint – both of the very best quality you can buy – a cloth, a paint product called Goldfinger (produced by one of our most famous paint firms) and, most important of all, your hands.

1. This is a cheap and fairly nasty, painted acanthus plaster candlestick – but the shape is good. To give it a look of wonderful old age, first spray-paint it with your good quality gold paint. Let this dry completely before spray painting it with matt black.

2. Put some rubber gloves on if need be, and with a cloth, while the black paint is still wet, wipe away as much as possible. The gilding beneath is revealed, and the black is still retained in the niches and crevices of the uneven surface. Let the black paint dry completely before going any further.

3. Using your tube of Goldfinger, squeeze a little on to your finger and smooth it on over the main gilded areas of the article you are working on. This, plus the natural oils from your hands, creates a wonderful patina, especially if, after the Goldfinger has been allowed to dry for about 30 minutes, you again rub it all over with your hands. You could buff it up with a fairly soft old shoe brush, or with a good duster, but I'm convinced it's the handling of the articles, the natural oils that come out of the hands, that gives this wonderful finish. The more you handle the objects you've 'antiqued', the nicer the patina becomes.

These candlesticks sit on my dining table at Christmas, and I have fooled many people into thinking they are quite old, medieval even! I hope that you will enjoy trying this, and all the other ideas in this chapter, and that they will all set your minds tingling with the possibilities of creating something splendid from virtually nothing.

Chapter Four

CRAFTY
COLLAGE
WORK

COLLAGE PICTURES

These are a joy to do, as they're so attractive if done well. I give very detailed instructions in general for the gold urn collage below, but there are many examples of collages I have created in the following pages (and throughout the book), and I hope that by examining and appreciating them, you will be fired with enthusiasm and want to take up the art yourself, to create your own.

Gold Urn Collage

1. First, prepare the backing board, here a rectangle of thin plywood. Cut a piece of fabric or paper – here maroon velvet – so that it measures approximately 4 cm (1½ inches) bigger all round than the backing board. Place it face down on the work table (wrong side up) and place the board on top. Glue a 4 cm (1½ inch) border all the way round the edge of the board. (Never apply glue to the *front* surface, as it might seep through the fabric.) Bring the fabric up from one side and press on to the glue, then pull fabric from the *opposite* side, and again press on to the glue. Repeat with the other two sides. At this stage, any creases will be pulled out, and you will have a smooth surface on which the collage can be built. Mitre the corners as in the illustration and in the *Tip* opposite.

2. Cut a neat piece of backing paper – wallpaper, brown wrapping paper etc – making it approximately 6 mm (¼ inch) smaller in diameter all round than the backing board. Glue round the edge of the paper and press on to the backing board so that the paper covers the edges of the fabric or paper covering the board. The whole thing should now look very neat.

T I P

To mitre the corners of a collage backing board covering – to neaten them – pinch the two upstanding edges together tightly at each of the four corners in turn. Press the bottom pieces into the glue, so that they are really firm. Using a good sharp pair of scissors, and working from the outside edge towards the centre of the backing, cut both 'ears' of fabric or paper through so that you are left with a neat mitred corner. Press down again on to the glue so that it all lies flat.

Commercial hangers can be bought from art shops and stores, but waste not, want not, say I, and the ring pulls from drink cans make ideal hangers. The 'tongue' is what is glued on to the back of the backing board, and the ring is the hanger. Apply glue to the tongue and press home firmly; leave for a couple of hours with a good weight on top so that it really does adhere. The backing board is now ready.

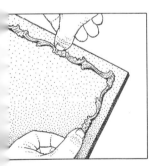

3. The backing board can, of course, be used by itself, or it can be put into a frame when finished (see page 86); or the impression of a frame can be created around the edges as here. I used the lightweight plastic trim available in DIY shops, sold to attach to wardrobe doors and dressing-table drawers etc. Gild this first (spray-paint with gold), then when dry, apply glue to the back of each piece and place carefully in position to create the frame effect. Now you are able to see and judge the area within which the collage is to be built. (Cord and lampshade braid can also be used to create this frame effect.)

In this particular instance, the gilded plastic urn was the first placement, as the collage 'arrangement' was to flow from this. The top outline – for height – was positioned,

and thus the shape and size of the group was determined,
the basic principle of all collages. Always leave space
between group and 'frame' because, as in flower
arrangements, the breathing space or the space left is just
as important as the space filled in.

4. At this stage, the outline is filled in, here with gilded
fern sprays, whirls of gold wire, sprays of pearl. Keep
the shape balanced on either side, but it mustn't look *too*
mechanically perfect – you're emulating to a great extent
the look of natural materials with artificial. Fill in
everything, overlapping slightly, to lead up to the final stage
of filling in the main area at the centre (again like in a
flower arrangement).

5. Now you can build up the 3-D focal point of the
group, and this is very important in all collages to
create interest. Wait until the first layer has dried, and then
build on top for a 3-D effect. Weight the ingredients down
if necessary. Here I used gilded linen flowers, pearlised cake
flowers, nylon tight leaves (see page 136), leaf cut-offs from
artificial ferns too small to use in arrangements (don't cut
up *new* sprays, use the bits at the bottom of your flower
boxes). I also included 15 pearls off a necklace threaded on
to wire to give a loop shape, and large pearls for round
shapes, with diamanté sprays and pearl stamens. Always use
different shapes and sizes, as well as textures, as it is the
variety of the collection displayed that makes the finished
collage interesting.

'Bacchus' Collage

This collage has become a great favourite of mine, with its centrepiece the lovely terracotta mask. As this was very heavy, I used the heavy ply as a backing and covered it with oatmeal linen.

As with all collages, the outline has to be created first. So, having placed the mask where I thought she ought to be, I marked around her with pencil. I then used epoxy resin to glue her in position. Then I tried things 'for size' to get the rhythm and movement I needed for the rest of the grouping. Starting from the right-hand side, I glued on some split bean pods from Kenya, and some cone shapes from Madeira. I wanted an almost Hawaiian flower look beside her ear, so made up a flower – the petals cut from dried banana leaves glued behind a teasel-shaped centre – and mounted that, along with other whirly pods, whirly bits of eucalyptus, and flower shapes, collapsed wood roses from the Caribbean.

Continuing down the left-hand side, I used another of those made-up flower shapes, and added proteas, lotus seed pods and broken cones, plus gourds and nut shapes to create that wonderfully bibulous and festive feeling the mask herself had originally suggested. As with any collage, you can be happy in general with the look of it, but there will be the odd place where a eucalyptus or laurel leaf – or even a skeletonised magnolia leaf – can be tucked in, just to give a very faint hint of something different.

When everything was completely set I gilded certain areas – the leaves and grapes around her head, the odd edge of a leaf, flower or lotus seed pod. I used Goldfinger (see page 72) and a fine paintbrush. This is just a *highlight*, though, so don't over-do it. It should look like something very old that has *lost* most of its gilding.

I called this my 'Bacchus' collage – all those grapes around the terracotta mask – but as I understand Bacchus was a feller, and she's so obviously female, she'll have to be Bacchus's sister! The materials that swirl so extravagantly about her are dried, and then I used Goldfinger to highlight just a few areas.

Green and Silver Collage

I wanted to show how something interesting could be created from items that cost virtually nothing (a common theme in this book, I think you'll have noticed!), and this collage is a good example. I already had the board, which is approximately 90 × 25 cm (3 feet × 10 inches), the velvet backing and silver lampshade braid for the 'frame', but the other items are virtually throw-outs.

To create the cascading curls and whirls, I used the pearls from an old necklace threaded on to wire (not genuine, and the clasp had broken). The round and butterfly shapes are in fact old belt buckles, again picked up for next to nothing – a shoebox of bits and pieces cost about 10p, I think. The filigreed leaf shape was cut from the edge of someone's wedding cake after the cake had been distributed. Other shapes are an odd pearl earring which has lost its friend, a few Maltese flowers from the Catholic shop (see page 86), and the hint of green – cut from a spray of velvet fern – which I knew would relieve and lighten the all-pearl-and-silver effect.

Brown and Gold Collage

The backing here is dark brown velvet edged with gold braid – both dull as I wanted to use quite bright and shiny cord to create the three lazy S-shapes. Do remember, as it is the differing surfaces and textures that create interest, never to use all shiny or all dull materials.

To create the S-shapes I pencilled around tin bottoms then joined them with the cord. Using gold doily pieces, odd Christmas leaves from the bottom of my boxes, gold beads and flower shapes – even the odd plastic shape, spray-painted gold – I sorted out three even lots of material for the three main areas. I placed them all as I wanted them, then, leaving one in position as reference, I glued on the other two, followed by the third. Remember to create the 3-D effect, as so many collages are flat and uninteresting. Make sure each level is set firm, then build another group on top.

A collage created, as so many things in this book are, from bits and pieces that cost virtually nothing.

This collage looks rather like an old-fashioned bell-pull. I used a brass curtain ring as hanger, attached by wire and staples, then surmounted it with a little gold bow — the final part of the grouping.

Black and White Collage

In my black and white hall there was a little stretch of wall that looked a bit empty, so I made this collage to fill it. I covered ply with black velvet paper, and created an outline using whirls of wired silver cord. Once I'd got the required shape and area, I then started to place on the flower and leaf shapes, ending with the main heart and weight of the group near the base, just like a flower arrangement.

The pearl flowers and little sprays I bought in the Catholic shop in Malta – an absolute hoard of treasures for people like me, I spent *hours* there. The flowers and sprays are made up into headdresses and used to trim the dresses of little girls being confirmed. Also playing their part here are little leaf and flower shapes cut from a piece of broderie anglaise – probably once part of a wedding or christening gown. There are also silver and white doily cut-outs, and some sprays of lily of the valley. The lovely pearlised leaves are also from Malta, and the butterfly is made from two pieces of broderie anglaise, with antennae made from wire with pearl ends. I then framed the collage as it was so delicate, having first added my initials. Well, painters and potters do it, why shouldn't I!

TIP

To frame a collage, you must lift the glass in your made or bought frame away from the 3-D or raised top of the collage work. Go to your local woodyard and buy some wood battening of about 4 cm (1½ inches) thick. Cover with the same backing fabric and make into a frame box shape. Glue this on to the backing of the collage, and then glue the whole thing into the frame.

All is not what it seems here. Many of the flower and leaf shapes – and the butterflies – are cut from broderie anglaise, or paper doilies, and the little sprays of lily of the valley are hand-made. They're silver wire with individually glued-on pearls (see page 123 for how to work with such tiny materials).

Cherub Collages

As you may have gathered, I never walk around with my eyes closed. I can see possibilities almost everywhere and in almost anything. We had decorated a bedroom in very pale soft colours and, because of a particular piece of furniture, wanted a pair of collages on either side of it, in the same pale colours, and long, thin and delicate. In the 'reject' department of a certain national concern selling bedroom and kitchen fittings, I found these two 'backings'. They are in fact white and pink drawer fronts, cost 10p each, and were just the job for the collages I wanted!

I also found two Italian wall cherubs which were hand-painted. These I glued in position with epoxy resin, weighing them down as in the *Tip* below. I pencilled in the sort of rhythmic outline I wanted, then glued on the various materials, having first sorted them out into two matching piles: you *must* work matching collages in tandem, with the same materials, for the best effect. I used gold coloured wire, tiny gold leaves, tiny pink and cream silk flowers, all coming up towards the feet and heads of the cherubs. I then used some small Christmas roses in linen, which I thought were the ideal flower for these groups. With the addition of some dark green silk foliage, the collages were just what I wanted.

TIP
I use some of my flatirons to weigh down heavier items in collage work. Lacking these, I suggest you use a house brick wrapped in newspaper.

When you're creating two matching arrangements, you have to sort your plant materials into two equal parts, and work them together. The same applies to two matching collages. Here I've used rather unusual backings – drawer fronts!

If you look back at some of the collages you can see how versatile they can be. The materials that are used are so different, that no two collages are ever the same.

DECORATING
WITH COLLAGE WORK

Once you've got into collages, you'll move on from pictures and want to decorate anything and everything. Apart from adding visually to your own home – or you – collage-decorated objects can be given as presents, which will be all the more appreciated because you've spent time and effort on them yourself. In the next few pages you'll get quite a few ideas of the possibilities!

Boxes

Mint and match boxes might not strike you as promising materials at first, but you can see here how good they look. The boxes to use are those with drawers rather than a lid that lifts: thus, every time you buy a new box, you can swap the drawer part over and put it into your decorated sleeve.

The top, after-dinner mint, box was covered with peachy velvet, with lampshade braid glued on to hide the selvedges. A group was glued on to the top – silver wires and leaves, gold fern shapes, the odd pearl earring and sprays of pearls. The mint stick box was done in more natural colours: covered with linen and braid edged again, with a central grouping of tiny dried flower heads, nut shell shapes and grass seed heads. The household match box is covered (avoiding the striker edge, of course) with brown suede, and edged with braid. The glamorous little grouping is made up with cut-outs from gold doilies, half an earring, some little gold leaves, and it is finished off with a bow of gold cord.

Another idea could involve tissue boxes. Cover them as above, carefully cutting and braiding around the edges of the tissue hole; with a little group on top, this too would make a marvellous present for somebody.

Boxes of mint chocolates make good presents to take to a dinner-party hostess, but if you cover the boxes with fabric and decorate them with collage work, they'll be even more appreciated! A household match box can be transformed in the same way.

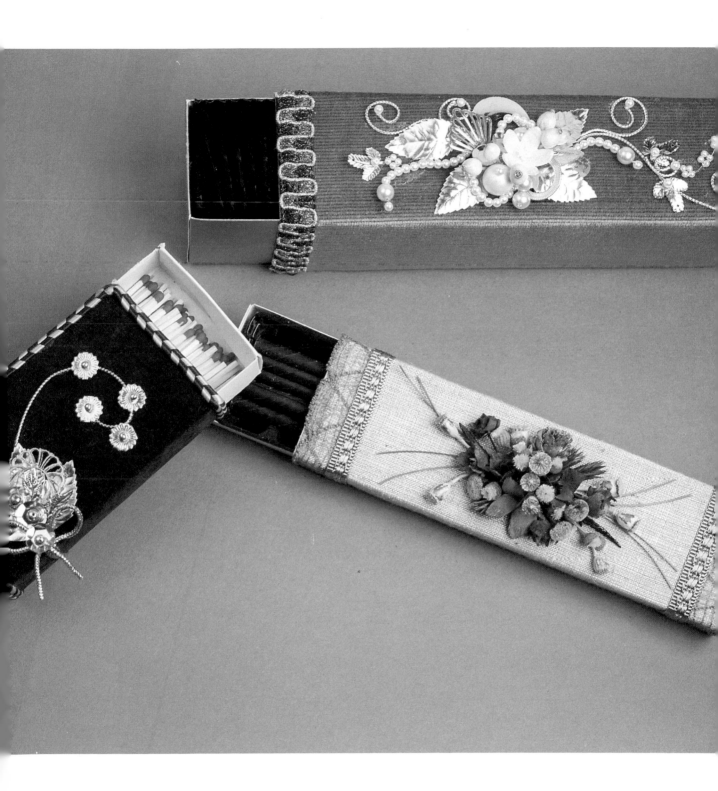

Baskets

Wicker baskets, hampers or boxes are not expensive to buy, and they are ideal to give as a present holding sewing materials, patchwork shapes to start someone off on yet another hobby, pretty little soaps or hand-made chocolates. If you decorate them with collage work, they'll look even more special.

On to the left-hand box, I glued a grouping composed of natural coloured dried flowers, cones and nut shapes. It was finished off with a nice little gingham bow (see page 138). The wicker hamper on the right had as its 'basis' a little bought basket shape cut in half. After this was glued in place, I 'filled' it with a profusion of small dried leaves, ferns, cone shapes and artificial fruits.

As with the boxes, you can decorate little baskets with collage work – in fact, it's easier, as you don't have to cover the basket with fabric first. Always remember though, in this type of work, to keep the proportions correct – small materials for small areas.

Bins

A bin such as this could also be a present, but it would look just as good in your own guest bedroom. You can either buy it naked and cover it with velvet and braid, or buy it already covered as I did, to save time. Choose a bin in an appropriate colour to suit the room you will put it in.

The collar of flowers here is simply a different way of interpreting collage work. It's still based on the same principles, and of course you could do a grouping on the side instead, if you preferred.

The flowers are silk and linen in pinks and blues, with some green silk foliage. When working on velvet as here, you'll need to apply the glue *twice*: let the first application all round the rim set, to create a coating, then apply more glue on top in the 10 cm (4 inch) sections that you'll be working on. Glue on your flowers and leaves, and then move on to the next 10 cm (4 inch) section, until you've worked your way right round the rim.

A different type of collage work, done as a collar around the top of a velvet-covered waste-paper bin. Choose the collage materials – here in silks and linens – to complement the velvet and the room for which the bin is being created.

Brushes and Hand Mirrors

I got the idea for these in a very exclusive shop in Paris, and again, a lovely idea for a present. Buy them new or, as I did, old but still very usable, in a local junk shop. (I sterilised the brush first, of course.) As the backs were looking a little seedy, I re-covered them with a peacock blue velvet and used a lampshade braid to cover the selvedges. To hide the join there's a little flower-shaped sequin.

I wanted these for a guest bedroom in tones of turquoise and peacock, so searched through my boxes for the odd bits and pieces that would create matching collage groups on the top. You'll recognise a few things here, I think – there are little gilded leaves, pieces cut from doilies, whirls of wire, old rings, the odd earring and pearl, with those turquoise shells. Anything in fact, that would give me the shapes and colours I wanted.

In a lovely little shop in Paris, we saw decorated hairbrushes, mirrors, tissue boxes, etc, and I thought I could do it too, as here. It just shows that, if you keep your eyes open, there is always an idea somewhere that can be utilised or adapted.

The idea of applying
objects to other objects —
the basic principle of
collage — is never-ending,
and I think it worked
particularly well in the
case of this comb. I've had
more comments about
these combs than anything
else, and the idea has
spread — I've seen quite a
few such decorated heads!

Hair Combs

My wife was going to a wedding and wanted something to
merely decorate her hair, rather than a hat. So, having seen
the price of combs like these in the shops, I determined to
make her one myself!

The combs are cheap to buy, and the additions are
treasures raided from my boxes again. As her dress was
midnight blue, I went for tones of that in my bits. I applied
a strip of epoxy resin glue along the head part of the comb,
and started off by laying on those gilded filigree leaves. In
the centre I glued on a cluster brooch of petrol blue beads
that had lost its middle. This was left for an hour weighted
down with my flatirons. I then applied further ingredients:
the little leaf shapes made from gold wire, and the deep
blue beads at the end, which were threaded on to wire
stems and glued on to the second layer of epoxy resin. The
final placements were the three gold beads with diamanté
centres.

Hats

I'm no David Shilling, but I have messed about with the
odd hat or two, mostly because I'm so involved with
weddings. Many brides and their attendants like to wear
hats instead of coronets and veils, particularly at a more
informal wedding, and I think the large straw hat here,
completely encrusted with peachy silk and dried flowers,
would be ideal for both bride or guest. All I did was to glue
flowers around (as for the bin) to create a collar, and
finished it off with a peach moiré bow (see page 138).

The other hats in the grouping have been worn by my
wife on various occasions. The hats are bought, but the
additions are by me. The cream one was bought to
accompany a peach, cream and black outfit, so I added
cream and peach silk flowers and a black velvet ribbon bow.
The black one with pearl and flower additions and sweeping
feathers was for a very special occasion. In 1979 I had the
very great honour of being the demonstrator for the
national NAFAS (National Association of Flower
Arrangement Societies) competitions, and I was on stage in
front of over 3,000 people in the Opera House in
Blackpool. I planned every last detail, even down to the
clothes that I and my two assistants wore: I wore a white
suit and a black shirt; they were all in black and topped
with these little nonsense hats. The pillbox 'bombes' were
bought, but I created the fantasy on top with the feathers
and the touches of cream and pearl.

The interesting thing about these little hat additions is
that they are not permanent. The groupings were made
using collage principles: they were glued on to card, any
visible card was cut away, then the card itself was pinned
on to the hat from underneath. With this idea, you can
ring the changes for any occasion!

*As you can see, there is
no end to the possibilities
of decorating with collage
work. Hats and shoes are
two fairly obvious
examples – and it's so
simple to dismantle the
decorations for either and
create a different group to
match yet another outfit.
Incidentally, all these
examples of 'domestic'
collage work are set
amongst a couple of
Victorian glass domes and
some of my wife's
collection of antique
hatpins.*

Shoes

Also in the hat picture overleaf are a pair of shoes which can be decorated in much the same way. These are my own daughter's wedding shoes, made of stiffened Spanish lace, and they had diamanté and pearl collages on the toes and down the backs of the heels. If the shoes are satin, say, you can build a grouping on to a piece of card and pin on as for the hats; if leather, and you don't want to pierce or glue them, use shoe clips on which you can build a group.

Bridal Headdresses

For a final thought on collage work that you can *wear*, I've done some on bride's and bridesmaid's headdresses. One of the biggest faults of these, I think, is the lack of back interest. The bridesmaid's coronet on the left is made of silk flowers and, on streamers flowing from the back of it, I've used the same, but very tiny, flowers, glueing them on in a collage group. The bride's headdress was worked on a comb (as on page 95), and includes a large blown rose, sprays of blossom, and those lovely trembling pearls on nylon wires. Cascading down from that are five ribbon streamers, on to which are glued little groups to match both headdress and bouquet. There are pearls, diamanté and little wax flowers, all of which help to keep the ribbons from flying all over the place. It's a good idea for a bride who doesn't want to wear a veil, but it looks just as good when acting as the *anchor* for a veil, as at my daughter's wedding in 1986. She wanted to walk up the aisle with her veil over her face — *very* traditional, of course — and this covered up one of the most magnificent headdresses I'd ever made. We still weren't happy about the little knot at the back where the veil came from, so this is how the streamer idea came into being!

I've always been an advocate of 'back interest' on bridal headdresses, as both bride and bridesmaid are mainly viewed from the back — during the service anyway. This streamer idea, with the tiny collage groupings on each ribbon, works very well, I think.

PRESSED FLOWER PICTURES

Pressed flower pictures (although too often they're *squashed*, in my view) utilise the same principles as collage work, and have been popular since Victorian times. The flowers are picked on a dry day, and immediately put in a book to start their pressing – an old telephone directory or, better, an old wallpaper book, with its absorbent papers. (Both these are infinitely superior to the squashing involved with actual presses.) Put a brick on top of the book and leave until well dried. I give a list of some of the best flowers for pressing on page 143.

In the photograph below you can see my pressed materials being taken from the wallpaper book and placed in tentative position on a sheet of paper, ready to be glued into place. The sharp scissors are vital for cutting, say,

Most pressed flowers are what I would call squashed, and I recommend that you use old telephone directories or, as here, wallpaper books, rather than commercial presses. Start at the end of the book, and fill it up, something between every page. When the material is ready, you can begin to arrange it, prior to glueing in place.

This pair of pressed flower pictures is displayed on a plain folding Victorian screen, which is a wonderful background for a variety of collages or pictures if wall space is limited. These pictures are 10 years old but all retain that lovely quality, as fresh as when originally created.

through the stems of things as here, to avoid the bunching together of stems in the finished picture. If you cover the 'hole' in the outline with a further layer of flowers, the flowers and stems will once again look completely natural.

In the pair of flower pictures attached to a Victorian screen (a good idea if space is limited), note the breathing space left between the group and the frame. Often there's so much material, it looks as though it's fighting to get out! I've used grasses, ferns and leaves, the easiest of all to press. There are clematis tendrils for rhythm and movement, potentillas, Japanese anemones, pansies, astrantia, sprays of mimosa and maple leaves. The butterflies are Victorian, the bodies hand-painted card, the wings real.

I think I've given you quite a few varied and different ideas on collage pictures and collage work. Gather together your bits and pieces and get sticking!

Chapter Five

CRAFTY CHRISTMAS

*Y*ou don't need me to tell you that it is at Christmas that the fingers, eyes and imaginations of flower arrangers can really come up trumps with crafty ideas. Everyone wants to decorate their houses colourfully and beautifully over the festive season, and there are so many ways in which to do so. I just *love* this time, and I love thinking up new ideas.

A Christmas welcome to your guests should begin right at the front door – and what better than a welcome ring. There are many different types available now, and you can have great fun decorating them. (In fact I love the idea so much that I hang rings on doors inside my house, covered or decorated with items I can live with the whole year round.)

Hanging decorations can always be used in a hall or room where space is limited, and of course there are many ideas you can adapt to hang from your Christmas tree. (There are a few further tree ideas in the next chapter which could play their part at Christmas.) Christmas collages, too, can be especially prepared, and they can brighten up a room in place of a more permanent picture.

Christmas is a wonderful time for kids, and they haven't been forgotten – they like beautiful things just as much as adults, whatever many people say. And Christmas gifts – well, you'll find a few ideas here, and throughout the book. Nothing pleases so much as something you have made yourself. The personal touch.

In the photograph on the previous page, you can see a wonderful selection from my collection of 'Fabergé' eggs and balls. This must be the ultimate in collage work, and how festive they look gathered together like this.

Christmas Materials

At this time, the materials used by crafty flower arrangers are in great abundance, manufactured here, imported from there. There are wicker, straw and twig rings and baskets, grass and herb bells, tinsel lengths, baubles, crackers,

wrapping papers, ribbons, some natural, some artificial –
and all in a plethora of colours. There's so much variety
that it's often very difficult to know what to choose.

You must very firmly bring all your artistic instincts to
bear on the planning. A rainbow of colours in your home –
or in one single arrangement – is never as successful as a
selected and select colour scheme. And as some Christmas
items can be so bright and brash, you need to use them
very carefully for the right effect. I would always go for the
limited colour scheme – all golds or silvers, or that
wonderfully festive combination of green and red. It's so
much more elegant.

Textures are important too. Many of the artificial
Christmas materials are made of plastic, and are very shiny,
so other textures must be included to offset these – fabric,
velvet, silk, glass or the gloriously natural textured look of
basket or wicker. The interest of any 'arrangement' lies in
the variety of shapes, textures and colours – a matt artificial
fern relieving the brightness of a gilded or lacquered item,
for instance – and so there must be contrasts. These can be
achieved too, of course, by the combination of natural and
artificial materials, which I've done successfully in a few of
the arrangements in the following pages.

But don't just think of Christmas materials having to be
bought. Many of the things you've craftily collected over
the years can be utilised in Christmas decorations – silk
flowers, baubles, bangles and beads, dried natural materials,
some of your foreign acquisitions, virtually anything that
has found its way into your storage boxes. And, as a final
thought, many of the ideas elsewhere in the book can be
adapted to Christmas use, as indeed many of the ideas
following can be adapted for use at other times of the year.

Have a happy, crafty Christmas!

WELCOME
RINGS

I've said on many occasions in the past and in many of my writings over the years that Christmas begins when you welcome people at your door. And *do* remember that they're not wreaths, they're welcome rings!

These rings come in such a wonderful array of materials now – polystyrene, bound twig, straw, oasis-filled, ribbon-bound – and you can see a selection from my collection below. There also are a few reels of ribbon, which are used with rings in bows (see page 138) and as hangers. The rings can be used outside or inside, depending on what additions you make, and can hang on door or wall. They needn't actually be used only at Christmas, of course. The one opposite is very Christmassy with its bright colours, but the step-by-step illustrations on the next page show how the idea can be utilised in autumnal colours, for a harvest or Thanksgiving celebration, for instance.

These welcome rings – not wreaths, please – used to be very difficult to obtain, and I had to haul them back from demonstration trips abroad. However, they have become increasingly available over the last few years, and in our shop at Christmas we must have had over 20 versions on offer. Ribbons, too, now come in a wondrous variety.

Christmas Twig Ring

In this natural bound twig ring, I have used a combination of natural and artificial materials. The first thing I did was to slightly buff up the ring with shoe polish to give it a gloss. Compare it with the one on the next page and you'll see what I mean. Turn there also for details of how to put it all together. Suffice to say here that I used corn and its stalks, brown ferns and cream Australian ferns to create the outline. The next placement was the red silk moiré bow (see page 138). The groups of artificial berries – looking good enough to eat – were clustered together for more impact and to be nearer the size of the glossy red apples, also artificial. Sprays of cones, poppy heads and little wooden fruits all create variety and interest. The green leaves are artificial foliage, and in the centre are two silk chlorophytum plants.

A Christmas welcome ring using a combination of natural and artificial materials, and in a colour scheme of creams, browns, reds and greens. The varied shapes add to the interest of the grouping, and the silk chlorophytum plants in the middle create an almost 3-D effect, as important in these rings as it is with collage work.

Autumn Welcome Ring

When using a beautifully bound twig ring such as this, one
of the basic ideas must be to show the ring itself as part of
the decoration. Therefore it is best to do an arrangement to
one side (a polystyrene ring is the one to use for a
completely circular arrangement). The materials used here
are all natural, and are all in natural, toning colours. I like
the tonings and variety through from the creams to the
very dark browns, but many people think they're rather
dead-looking, and would prefer some colour. If you do
want to add colour, stick to just one or two that tone:
multi-coloured just aren't as successful!

1. Tape a square piece of drifoam on to the ring with
floral foam tape. The first placements are a group of
cream-coloured grasses and pheasant feathers. A lot of
people dislike using the latter, but why, as they add interest
and a different texture to the grouping. The grasses look
quite natural, I think, just as though a lovely bunch had
been collected and laid across the ring – but they haven't
been, see the *Tip* below.

T I P

A block of drifoam would break up if lots of grass stalks,
or the thick stems of bulrushes or reeds, were pushed
through it. The answer is to cut the ends of the stalks
off, and arrange the stalks and the main heads *separately*
in the drifoam. They *look* natural, but there are two
totally separate group placements. (Basically the same
principle as employed in the pressed flower picture on
page 100.)

2. After getting the flowing line across the ring, the next placement is the bow of ribbon. See page 138 for how to make these. I wanted the bow to look as though it was holding the collected group together on the ring, and chose a linen Kashmir pattern ribbon which comes in wonderful colour combinations. After that comes the foliage for the arrangement – some rather nice cocoa brown sea grape leaves from Florida. These are very useful not only because of their colour and size, but they also help, if properly placed, to hide the mechanics. Also added now are some whirl-topped canes (bought like this) and whirls of open pea pods, again picked up on a foreign trip. Both give the rhythm, movement and variety needed.

3. Towards the centre are some groups of wooden fruits which, on a stem, look rather like a bunch of grapes. Alongside them are the lovely open pods of dried eucalyptus flowers, large pine cones, and some poppy heads.

Red Welcome Rings

This particular group of rings would create a really festive welcome. I bought them already lacquered, but you can lacquer your own (see the *Tip* below) very successfully.

When working with non-natural looking bases such as these rings, you must choose your 'ingredients' very carefully. You can continue the colour and the gloss, but you mustn't *over*-do it. The four apples on the large ring and one each on the smaller rings were just right. I've used velvet ferns and a plastic grey yew foliage so that there are contrasts between the gloss and the more matt ferns and leaves. It's these contrasts which make all the difference.

Start by working first on the small rings. Attach the small pieces of drifoam and insert the small fern shapes, the tiny berry sprays, the apple and finally the red velvet bow (see page 138). Use more velvet ribbon, in varying lengths, to suspend these small rings from the large one.

Attach the drifoam to the large ring, and insert the larger pieces of fern to the sides, then slot in the yew at the top. Use long and short sprays of the berries, and smaller fern pieces, to recess into the middle before you insert the focal point, the red apples. The last placement should be the large red bow, and then you can hang the welcome rings up, either from another length of ribbon, or from a nail on to which the weave of the ring is pushed.

This jolly red welcome ring 'arrangement' should bring a smile to the faces of anyone ringing your doorbell at Christmas.

TIP

If you can't find lacquered welcome rings, lacquer your own. Simply buy a can of car spray paint – preferably in a cheerful Christmas colour – and spray the ring lavishly on all sides until completely coated. If an old lacquered or other ring ever looks a little seedy, a re-spray will brighten it up again.

Welcome Ring Table Arrangement

Welcome rings are very versatile and need not necessarily be hung from a door. They could also be used horizontally, and indeed this is more like the traditional Advent usage in Europe, where the rings are suspended 'flat' in a window, and hold four candles for the four Sundays of Advent. However, the rings can also be used as a table decoration.

Once again the rings (I've used two) are made of roughly bound twig. The larger ring sits very neatly on any piece of furniture, and the small ring (which sits on top and holds the group) was wired on to the lower one with large hairpins of florists' wire for stability. The first placement was, as usual, the piece of drifoam to take the three candles. Use the plastic floral foam candleholders (available at floral accessories shops) or my tripod idea in the *Tip* below. Push into the drifoam to allow the candles to stand perfectly stable and safe. (Remember to have the candles at different heights for interest.)

Next, insert the outline foliage – here variegated silk ivy – and, depending on the size of the area to be decorated, it can trail effectively out to the sides. As it's a Christmas decoration, I've then used silk poinsettias, fruits and pine cones as well as a large red velvet ribbon bow. All of these should be recessed carefully to cover the drifoam: a table arrangement will be viewed quite closely. You could also use fresh materials if you liked.

A welcome ring holding Christmas flowers, foliage and candles would make a wonderful hall-table arrangement with which to greet your guests. It would look good too on a side table in your Christmas dining room. The hanging arrangement is described on page 114.

T I P

A candle pushed into floral foam or drifoam would make a huge hole. Instead, make tripod legs for the candle. Tape three cocktail sticks (or wooden skewers for larger candles) to the foot of the candle and these will slot into the foam securely.

HANGING DECORATIONS

Decorations which hang look lovely at Christmas in your hall (or outside if appropriate, like a winter hanging basket), but one of their main advantages is that they take up very much less space than a decoration sitting on a table. And there are so many variations on the theme.

Hanging Rods

The glamorous idea in the previous photograph may appeal to you, as a start. I got the lovely striped silver and red glass rods (they're probably Victorian) from a friend who ran the display department of a store, and was having his ten-year spring-clean. I don't know their original purpose, but I thought them ideal for a hanging decoration so long as I could devise some means of attaching an arrangement. Drifoam didn't work, but I eventually hit upon collars of plasticine, and built up a group with lovely red velvet ferns, whirls of wired silver cord, silver flowers, baubles and bells. In the absence of glass rods, why not adapt the idea, using long pieces of wood dowelling, either painted or ribbon wrapped. Just put the thinking cap on.

Herb Bell

These wonderful bells come from Spain, and are made from grasses bound into shape with dried herbs.

Again, so that you can still see the shape, I did the arrangement on the top. In the hook or handle part, I wedged a piece of drifoam and then attached the hanging pink hessian ribbon and the bow. Pink was my chosen colour, and I used a combination of natural materials – dried helichrysum, various seed heads, grasses, leaves and larkspur – and non-natural, the sprays of silk blossom.

The materials used here aren't actually Christmas
materials, but I wanted to show the possibilities for other
times of the year (as with the autumnal welcome ring) –
but just imagine it with sprays of holly, some of those lovely
shiny red apples, and a red velvet bow. This is a summer
grouping here, but you could give it a few weeks' rest, then
decorate it for autumn with sprays of corn, pine cones,
dried gourds and some helichrysum.

These herb bells smell
wonderful, particularly as
a room warms up.
Although the flowers used
here are summer
materials, think how good
it would look adapted for
Christmas with Christmas
plants and colours.

Children's Basket

Many people think children don't care for 'flower' arrangements, but I'm quite convinced they do. Whether you are a child of 9 or 90, I'm sure you would appreciate something like the hanging basket here. And the idea is so adaptable.

The bound twig basket had a very shallow cavity, but into this I fixed my piece of drifoam and the gingham bow to match the ribbon hanger. Then I went to town with my materials, all with wires or sticks attached. The lollipops have their own sticks, wooden satay sticks are threaded into the crackers, the little parcels have their own wires – they're Christmas tree decorations – as have the teddy bears. I added a tiny amount of fern foliage simply to make it look a little more natural.

Poppy Heads

This is one of the most interesting ideas I've come up with of late, and it came quite by accident. I wanted to decorate my tree with completely natural things, but something dangly was missing, thus the poppy heads.

These are very large Continental ones, not all that easy to find. I attached a cord hanger to a pin with some glue on it, and pushed the pin into the stem part. I then put a ring of glue around the top and started gluing on my tiny bits: pieces of treated gypsophila (Bristol fairy), gold baubles, and plastic fruit. The latter were first coated with glue and then rolled in seeds – grass, herb or poppy – to get that knobbly effect. I've also got bound sticks of cinnamon which give a lovely aroma, and a little velvet bow.

Similar to my hanging Christmas pine cones, these Continental poppy heads can be decorated in much the same way, with a collar of collage work around the top. Keep to a limited colour scheme – natural browns, golds and creams as here, or reds and greens or golds and greens.

Christmas and children (of whatever age) just go together, and this hanging basket idea should appeal. Why not do one for each member of the family, filling them with different types of materials?

CHRISTMAS COLLAGES

I expect you thought you'd seen the last of collages! However, they can make a substantial contribution to Christmas cheer. Turn to page 78 for the basic details of making.

The red shield collages are very cheery, I think. The shield shape was cut from hardboard, covered in a ribbed linen, and edged with gold cord; gold tassels hang at the bottom, and the collages are suspended from gilded curtain tie-backs with those red bows (see page 138). The central medallions are small cherub-encrusted plaster picture frames, and there are gold cherubs in the middle. Beneath are whirls of gold cord, leaves and flowers. The 'mythical birds' flying in at the top were made from gilded natural materials – layers of leaves, cane flicked along the back of a knife – and they were built on to pieces of cardboard (most of which was cut away before the birds were glued into place).

To finalise this Christmas idea, I've returned to the children. I was asked by the Yorkshire Flower Club to do a pair of collages on the theme 'Once Upon a Time', and it was quite difficult to think up. However, Mary Poppins popped into my head, and I think it works very well. A deep purple background was the start, then I worked in pinks, blues and purples. Some of the materials are bought, some made up. I didn't actually want a Mary Poppins figure, but these fan shapes covered in pink and muted velvets started her off – they're copies of Victorian Christmas tree decorations, as are the little maroon hat boxes and baubles. The baubles I cut in half, as I did the little baskets glued there too (as on page 92), into which I put groups of little flowers. The white shapes are pipecleaners.

I made these red shield collages for a flower festival in Ripon Cathedral, and I bring them out at Christmas, replacing year-round pictures, and bringing colour and variety during the festive weeks.

The children would enjoy a collage such as this, with its Victorian feel and the evocation of Mary Poppins floating along on her brolly. The little halved baubles and baskets give an interesting 3-D effect, and the flowers in the baskets have slight movement as people walk past – almost as though Mary were offering them to you!

FABERGÉ WORK

One of the greatest influences on my decorative work has been Peter Carl Fabergé (1846–1920), the Russian goldsmith. He made many wonderful *objets d'art* in precious metals and stones for the Imperial Court of Russia, as well as other royalty. His most famous creations were the jewelled Easter eggs he made for the tsars to give the tsarinas on Easter morning, each one containing a surprise gift, but he also made animals and flowers, boxes, picture frames and scent bottles. To me his work includes some of the most beautiful and desirable objects in the world.

Quite a lot of my collage work is inspired by Fabergé – the tin boxes in the *Flower Arranger's Bible*, and indeed the boxes on page 90. However, the egg idea started me off on my own Fabergé egg collection, a few of which you can see opposite and on pages 102–103. I think you'll have to agree that these must be the ultimate in collage work. They're fun to do and not really difficult, and they would make wonderfully decorative objects in your own home, and absolutely splendid gifts for Christmas.

The basis is a polystyrene egg or ball shape, and they're first covered in lush velvet (see page 122). Most of the bead or other decoration is attached to the shape with a pin – rather like those First World War pincushions made by servicemen – but some bits need to be glued on. The designs on the eggs can be as elaborate or as simple as you like. The materials used must complement the colours of the velvet and of the braid, and I prefer to do alternate panels, or *each* panel, depending on the style or lavishness of the decoration. Some eggs have one large motif on one side, the green one in the left forefront, for instance, which was my first effort. The materials can be various, too, but the more glamorous the better.

Each egg or bell has a finial top with spectacular decorations, as you can see. These can be a number of things – gold or silver wire loops, beads, buttons, brooches or earrings. The brown and silver egg on the palm tree stand on pages 102–103 (a candleholder which looks much more effective with an egg in it) has swirls of wired pearls which are pinned into the polystyrene and topped with an antique pearl hatpin.

Each egg rests on some sort of stand: candleholders, special egg stands available from craft shops, or a brass curtain ring with four pearls glued on to make the feet.

If you like the idea – and I hope you do – all I can say is 'happy egging'!

Do display your 'Fabergé' eggs and balls effectively: although they could be hung on nylon thread from a tree or branch, I think they would lose a lot of their detail.

Covering Fabergé Eggs and Balls

The egg or ball shapes in Fabergé work first need to be covered in velvet, the basis for the decorations to be applied. But obviously the shapes cannot just be *wrapped* in the fabric; this would create folds and bumps, and you need a smooth surface. What you do is cut the fabric into petals – six of them – and you'll need to make paper templates for this. Don't worry, it's not difficult, particularly if you follow my instructions and look at the illustrations.

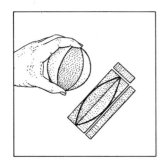

1. To measure the length and circumference of the polystyrene shape, look at the paper shapes to the left. Cut a long piece of paper about 1 cm (½ inch) wide. Mark the length from top to bottom of the shape on the paper and cut. Then go round the circumference of the shape and mark that on the paper strip. Divide this latter measured strip into six by folding then cutting. The long strip records the length of the petal from top to bottom; the small strip marks the width of each petal, one-sixth of the circumference. Cut a piece of paper to this exact width and length, and fold it in half lengthwise. Pencil and then cut a curved line from one end of the fold to the other, and open out into the paper petal template. This curves beautifully around the shape – as will the velvet once you have cut it out too.

2. Lay the template against the wrong side of the velvet, and mark around it with pen or pencil. Do this six times for each shape, and then cut out. To fix the petals to the shape, find a glue that does not affect the polystyrene: many are available in craft shops, but if all else fails, use polystyrene tile paste. Coat half the shape with the glue and let it become slightly tacky before carefully

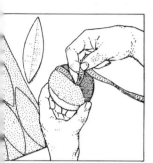

sticking on three of the petals. Making sure your hand is meticulously clean, hold on to the covered half while you glue and then cover the second half.

3. Your petals may not meet, or may overlap – but don't panic! Each join is covered with braid (I have occasionally used lace, ribbon, cord or strings of pearls) which completely disguise any errors. Pin the end of the braid on at the top with a short straight dressmaker's pin, and stretch it completely down one join as here until you get back to where you started. Cut and pin. Do this three times to cover the six joins, and using two to three pins only. Your shape is now neat, and ready for all your materials to be pinned – or indeed glued – on. What could be easier?

A crafty Christmas indeed. Hope you enjoyed it.

T I P

Many very small things in this type of work are difficult to handle if you want to glue them on to the surface. What I do is thread a bead on to one pin, then put a drop of glue on the point, on to which the bead slips and is held. I then place the beaded pin over the desired position and push the bead off with another pin. The bead takes the glue off with it, and sticks in exactly the right position. (With unholed tiny things, you'll need to use tweezers, and have a very light hand with the glue.)

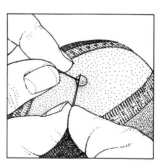

Chapter Six

SILK CRAFT
PLUS

*T*he photograph on the previous page shows me in our shop in Yorkshire, surrounded by the various things we sell for people interested in flower arranging. These 'things', however, are not *fresh* flowers: they are silk and polyester flowers, dried flowers, and many containers, baskets, rings and other flower-arranging accessories, all part of the crafty flower arranger's art.

Silk and Dried Flowers

Artificial flowers, you may ask, what is Derek Bridges coming to – but there is artificial and there is artificial. Some of the silk or polyester flowers we sell are so realistic, that people bend to sniff them, and cannot believe that they are not fresh. Perhaps their deceptive qualities can best be summed up in a comment I overheard in the shop: 'They're good enough to be plastic'!

The flowers that started it all off were probably those plastic roses given away – in the fifties? – with a brand of washing powder. Artificial flowers have come a long way since then and, although many flower arrangers would not dream of giving them house room, *I* would, and do.

I always buy the best, however, and I must recommend that you do the same. You pay for quality, of course, but they will last for ever if you take care of them. Even silk flowers need a rest every now and then – and I wouldn't want to live with *one* arrangement of them for longer than about six weeks. (This is where they get a bad name – in the one arrangement year in, year out, having the dust blown off every second Thursday.) Arrange, enjoy, then dismantle and pack away in a large cardboard flower box (not polythene as they can go limp). Clean them every so often with a very soft, clean paint or pastry brush; some people use a hairdrier on a very low speed.

(Previous page) In the photograph of the interior of my shop you can begin to appreciate, I think, the wealth of materials – silk, linen, polyester, dried, natural, artificial – that is available to us flower arrangers.

One way of organising this cyclical use of silk or polyester flowers is to use them seasonally, in seasonal arrangements. When they first became popular, they were often used in arrangements in hotels, pubs, hairdressers' and banks, with all the seasons jumbled together. What did it matter that summer roses, chrysanthemums and daffodils were all in together, they filled a gap. Thank goodness that people today have more taste. A spring selection can give way to a summer selection, and these flowers come completely into their own towards the end of the year, when fresh flowers are less accessible, and when the central heating so inimical to fresh is in full flow. Dried flowers are useful then too.

Silk and dried flowers can be used by themselves in traditional arrangements, both glamorous and more homely, but they can also be used together. Mixing artificial fruits, foliages and flowers with fresh materials can also be interesting. Say, for instance, you were doing the flowers for a wedding and, as always, to a budget. If some large lilies would just finish off the job, and fresh are not available, too dear or too tightly budded, use silk – they'll look super. (If entering competitions, though, be careful about the use of silk with fresh – read the rules carefully.) Both artificial and dried materials can also be used decoratively in many other ways, as you'll see (and will already have seen).

The Crafty Pluses

Making a bow from ribbon is one of the skills you *must* acquire, as bows are useful in so many aspects of crafty flower arranging. You'll learn here how to create them, as well as further artifices – how to make flowers and blossoms from the most unlikely materials.

DECORATING
BASKETS

———

Most of you will know how fond I am of basketwork, and
my collection of varying types must now exceed 200. For
flower arrangers baskets themselves are a mine of
possibilities as they can be used in so many ways, inside or
outside in the garden (see page 31). I've already described
how basketwork or wicker boxes can be decorated with
collage work (see page 92); here I thought I'd demonstrate
how silk and dried flowers can be used in conjunction with
baskets. You don't always have to do an arrangement *inside* a
basket, there are other 'surfaces' such as the rim and the
handle.

Valentine Basket

This would make an ideal gift for any young lady on the
14th February, perhaps filled with home-made chocolates or
pot-pourri.

1. The basket is made of twig and you can see how easy it
will be to bind flowers on to that open-weave rim. I
chose pink as my colour scheme, and there are roses,
heathers, narcissi and blossom, with foliage in between, all
in silk.

2. Starting at the top of the heart, and using florists'
wire, I laid the first rose, narcissus and piece of
blossom on the rim. I led the piece of wire through the top
twigs of the rim to bind the little grouping on. I then
continued with the next grouping, laying on, binding,
laying on, and binding.

3. I worked my way completely down one side of the heart, then added a ribbon bow at the top (see page 138) and started down the other side, from the top, until the whole rim was bound with colour. A very simple idea, but one which is amazingly effective and pretty.

Twig Basket

This too is made of twigs, but it is finer, and has a lovely high handle and flowing sides. The empty centre can, as before, be used for pot-pourri or something similar – a wonderfully decorated and scented 'arrangement' for any room – and again, would make a delightful gift. I actually hung this on the wall in my shop where it looked very good.

I used both silk and dried materials for this rim, and bound them on with raffia (why *is* this so difficult to find now?). All the stemmed dried items were cut to about 10–12 cm (4–5 inches), and I added wire stems where necessary. I bound items on in clusters, overlapping them to get that rich profusion, using anything for variety, interest and a talking point. The final additions were two silk bows (see page 138).

I decorated the rim of this basket, using dried helichrysums, poppy heads, statice, cut cones which give that rose shape, large leaves, corn and grasses, and some lovely pieces of dried fungus. There are also some pink silk blossoms. The final additions were two silk bows (see page 138).

It was the handle of this rope basket that I chose to decorate, and I used silk and linen flowers, blossoms, roses and daisies. There's a bunch of artificial frosted grapes there too, with a ribbon bow as the final touch.

Rope Basket

Here the handle rather than the rim has been decorated, and the beauty of the actual basket itself is fully revealed, leaving the cavity completely free for chocolates, fruit or, as here, some biscuits made by my daughter Sara. Once again, a lovely present for a special occasion.

A handle arrangement could be made into a taped-on piece of drifoam or a large knob of plasticine. I actually wedged a piece of styrofoam in between the two pieces of rope handle, then fixed it with floral foam tape. Once again the flowers are silk and linen, with a bunch of artificial frosted grapes and a ribbon bow.

BLOSSOMS
AND 'BONSAI' TREES

We've had two bonsai trees in our married life and both
died after about a year, so I thought I'd have a go at
'bonsai' trees that lasted a little longer. Thus my tree shapes
– basically interesting branches – with 'blossom' applied to
them. These blossoms can be silk as below, plastic (as on
page 50), or made up from items as diverse as pistachio nut
shells (see page 68), wax matches, sugared almonds, or
nylon tights! I've even used those polystyrene sheets that
hold boxed apples: if you cut petal shapes, attach wires and
stamens of wired beads, you end up with a wonderful
waterlily. You can also make magnolia buds and flowers –
paint with white emulsion if you can only find blue or
green polystyrene – and those would look wonderful on
that 'bonsai' branch on page 67.

*A 'bonsai' branch of
contorted hazel (you could
use willow) is fixed into a
piece of 'swathed'
soapstone. The blossoms
were cut from a spray of
silk flowers, and glued on
with a few silk leaves.
Very natural and very
simple.*

A 'bonsai' tree is created from a piece of Kenyan thorn and a few almond flowers. Note the shell used as an accessory, its mother-of-pearl sheen complementing the flowers and the base.

Almond Flowers

The idea for these came when I saw some sugared almonds scattered after a party. Flowers, yes, but how to attach a stem to them? I didn't want to use glue, or to pierce the sugar coating, so I came up with clingfilm. Each almond is covered in a piece with surplus at one end; this is screwed up into a 'stem'. The flowers as you can see, are made from five clingfilm-covered almonds with a centre: this could have been another sweet, virtually anything in fact, but I chose to use three pearls on silver wires. The clingfilm stems and the wires were then wired together to make the flower.

The 'bonsai' idea was utilised once more. As I wanted subtle, pearly colourings, I arranged the shell and the piece of Kenyan thorn tree on a pearl-grey base. The almond flowers are wired on to the branch, and almonds spill out of the shell. (These flowers also have possibilities in collage work, on top of boxes as on page 90.)

Sugared almonds come in pretty pastel colours and, wrapped in clingfilm, they can be made into spectacular flowers.

133

Matchstick Flowers

The idea for these came from a friend of mine in Spain, and I think it's one of the most novel I've ever encountered in my world of flower arranging. The basis of the flower petals is a wax match – those matches you get given in foreign hotels and bars!

You might think using matches is slightly dangerous, especially when the heads are looped together as opposite, but they are safety matches, which only strike on the box and not against each other.

Follow the detailed – but very simple – instructions in the captions below and continue until you have made the required number of flowers – or have run out of matches. Simply glue the back of each flower and stick it in place on your branch or tree.

Matchstick flowers look spectacular on a contorted hazel 'bonsai' branch in a black lacquered container. To hide the pinholder, I used a couple of stones and some shattered windscreen glass for that shimmer.

1. Take a wax match and unfurl it – it's made from rolled-up wax paper. Open it out completely, taking care not to knock off the striker head.

2. Holding the striker head, take your sharp scissors and carefully cut the end of the wax paper into a petal shape, curving around as in the drawing.

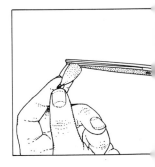

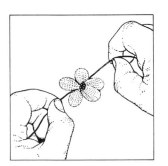

3. Make five petals for every flower, then lie the petals down flat on the table, turning the striker heads so that they point upwards. Arrange the five heads together in the centre of the petals and, with a piece of nylon thread, strong cotton or fine silver wire, make a loop and lasso the five heads together. Tie the wire or thread tightly, cut off any surplus, and the flower is ready.

Nylon Tights Flowers

Flowers have been made out of all sorts of objects over the years. The Victorians, for instance, used paper, leather and shells – you name it, they used it – but however creative they were, they couldn't have thought of my next 'ingredient'. The flowers in the arrangement below are made, literally, from ladies' nylon tights. These come in all sorts of thicknesses, textures and colours, and they can be extremely effective, as you can see.

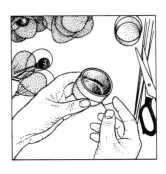

1. You need wire that will hold its shape when you stretch the nylon over it. I use 22 gauge florists' wire. Make the basic petal shape by winding your wire around something round, twist the legs together, and remove. Make quite a few such petal shapes – five to ten for each flower, and perhaps of different sizes for interest.

2. Take the chosen pair of tights and push the wire shape inside. Be economical, starting at the foot or the top, so that you can use as much of the nylon as possible. Stretch the nylon over the wire, and once you are happy with it, wind another piece of wire round the petal stem two to three times catching the nylon and making it firm. Cut off the surplus nylon. Continue doing this to make all the petals you require.

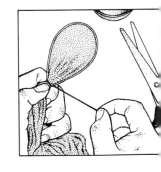

3. For the flower centre I've used a wire-stemmed bauble, the same colour as the nylon. Gather three petals together with the bauble, and twist the wire around at the stem end.

4. Attach the remaining petals – I've used another seven here – and twist wire around the stems to hold the flower firmly together. Move the petals gently into the required position, and your flower is virtually ready. Add a longer wire stem if necessary, and twist floral stem tape around it, if you like, to disguise the wire.

I think it would be difficult for most people to guess what the flowers here are made of, looking so spectacular in and beside a black wine bottle with a few pieces of black-painted twig. They're actually made from ladies' nylon tights!

RIBBON BOWS

In the photograph of welcome rings on page 106 you can also see a few reels of ribbon, illustrating some of the wonderful colours, fabrics and textures that ribbon comes in nowadays. I love ribbons, and I use a lot of them in my work – as binding, as braiding, as hangers, on headdresses and, mostly, in ribbon bows. These are useful in all sorts of decorations and arrangements.

To make sure that you can make one without any hesitation, doubt or mistakes, follow the steps below very carefully.

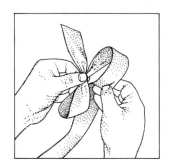

1. All bows have two tails, long or short as you please. To make a bow of approximately 20 cm (8 inches) across, get your ribbon and pinch it 10 cm (4 inches) from the end between the finger and thumb of your left hand (right, if you're left-handed). This is one of the tails. Taking the bulk of the ribbon, make a loop of about 10 cm (4 inches) long and bring it back to the same pinching finger and thumb. I've just about made my second loop here, and you go on making these loops, pinching them each time, until you've got as many as you want.

2. Leave a tail to match the first one, and cut the ribbon. Here you'll see I've got four loops only, with two tails. Take a piece of florists' stub wire and put it across where you've been holding on with finger and thumb, to catch all the loops. Bring the two legs together underneath, to create that hairpin shape, and trap the loops. Twist the legs together, to hold the loops firmly. Tweak each loop into a good curving shape.

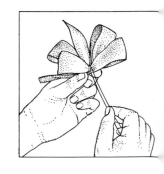

From the colour photograph you will see how you can vary this basic theme. The red velvet bow is the one I've just made. The Christmas bow at the foot consists of two of these velvet bows bound together and topped with what is known as a Christmas pick – a little group of artificial foliage, baubles and a parcel – a wonderful bow to decorate a Christmas present. The bow at top right is composed of two simple bows of different fabrics – yet another possible effect. And the glamorous one at top left uses some of my favourite Kashmir ribbon in a large bow topped with a second smaller silk one, and then a lovely cluster of dried flowers, painted cones, fruit shapes, foliage and a little parcel. This too could go on a gift wrapping, but it would also look good attached to a Christmas tree or either end of a Christmas garland, on the staircase or above the mantelpiece.

Once you learn how to make a bow properly, there's no end to their decorative uses.

SILK FLOWER
ARRANGEMENTS

To prove how magnificent silk materials can look, I show here two contrasting arrangements – one glamorous, and one more homely, for the kitchen.

The hanging wicker basket – rather like a mini hayrack – holds a collection of wooden and wicker spoons, mallets, kebab skewers and a fork. The colours are wonderful, toning with the wicker. A piece of drifoam was wedged into the basket, and wooden satay skewers taped to the bottoms of the implements (a tripod as in the *Tip* on page 112). These implements created the outline along with some silk foliage, a bunch of grass stems tied together with a gingham bow, sprays of ivy and some large silk dieffenbachia leaves. To bring colour to the centre, I used two silk wild strawberry plants. A couple of dried gourds, and some dried

In another of my crafty home-made containers, I arranged a summer profusion of the most beautiful silk flowers. I don't think that even the most hardened 'anti-silk' person could deny their magnificence.

In this hanging basket arrangement for the kitchen, I used some of my collection of wooden implements, plus natural and dried materials, and a number of silk items – ivy, dieffenbachia, and wild strawberry plants, with foliage, fruit and blossom together.

fungus were added, along with a bunch of aromatic cinnamon sticks, bound together with a tiny matching bow.

The figurine container I virtually made. She looked a bit sad when I bought her, so I glued some flower and fruit shapes to her basket where it was most battered, and then 'antiqued' the whole thing (see page 72). I then made a plinth to hold the flower container; a catering size coffee tin with some cement weight inside and a hole drilled in the top edge to take a metal rod with a flat top. This was a couple of parts of an old millinery hatstand, upside down. A container was glued to the former bottom of the hatstand at the now top of the rod. The coffee tin was covered in velvet and braid, and the figurine merely placed alongside the gilded metal rod.

The flowers are ferns, irises, hollyhocks, delphiniums, roses, peonies, lilies and poppies, all the sorts of things which give us the glories of a summer garden – but in silk.

Well, I hope you have enjoyed my ideas and now it's up to you to be as crafty as me.

SOME PLANTS FOR PRESSED PICTURES

Flowers
Anemone
Astrantia
Broom
Buttercup
Celandine
Clematis
Clover
Cow Parsley
Daffodil
Daisy
Delphinium
Golden rod
Heather
Honeysuckle
Hydrangea
Marigold
Mimosa
Pansy
Poppy
Potentilla
Rose

Grasses
Mouse tail
Trembling grass
Wild barley

Ferns
Common polypody
Japanese holly
Maidenhair

Leaves
Ash
Beech
Blackberry
Cineraria
Clematis
Helleborus
Honesty
Ivy
Maple
Oak
Prunus
Senecio
Whitebeam

SOME ALPINE PLANTS FOR CONTAINER GROWING

Achillea *rupestris* (yarrow)
Alyssum *spinosum*
Androsace *helvetica* (rock jasmine)
Anemone *blanda* (windflower)
Campanula *arvatica* (bellflower)
Campanula *raineri*
Cyclamen *neapolitanum*
Dianthus (pinks and carnations)
Eranthis *hyemalis*
Euphorbia *myrsinites*
Gentiana (gentian)
Hypericum (St John's wort)
Leontopodium *alpinum* (edelweiss)
Potentilla *verna* 'Nana' (cinquefoil)
Primula *denticulata*
Saxifraga (many)
Sedum (many)
Spiraea *hendersonii*

SOME PLANTS FOR GARDEN CONTAINERS

Aucuba japonica (spotted laurel)
Begonia
Buxus (box)
Cotoneaster
Cupressus (cypress, slow-growing types)
Dwarf conifers
Euonymus (spindle tree)
Geranium
Hedera (ivy, all types)
Herbs
Hosta (plantain lily, all types)
Hydrangea
Ligustrum (privet, all types)
Pelargonium
Polyanthus
Pot chrysanthemum
Sedum
Senecio
Skimmia
Spring bulbs
Vinca (periwinkle)

INDEX